EUROPEAN JOURNAL OF DEVELOPMENTAL PSYCHOLOGY
2008, 5 (5), 537–543

 Psychology Press
Taylor & Francis Group

Introduction: Developmental co-construction of cognition

Christine Sorsana

University of Toulouse 2, Toulouse, and University of Nancy 2, Nancy, France

Since the 1970s, a large number of experimental studies (see, for example, Gilly, 1995; Hinde, Perret-Clermont, & Stevenson-Hinde, 1985; Light & Butterworth, 1992; Perret-Clermont & Nicolet, 2001; Sorsana, 1999, 2001) as well as ethnomethodological observations of everyday cognition (Lave, 1992; Schliemann, Carraher, & Ceci, 1997) have brought out the fact that social interaction influences cognitive development. However, a crucial question remains: what is the true nature of this influence?

Whereas the debate on the relationship between social interaction and cognition is not very evident in contemporary research in cognitive psychology of development and reasoning (Barrouillet, 2007; Blaye & Lemaire, 2007; Markovits & Barrouillet, 2004; Politzer, 2002; Siegler, 1998), with the exception of some work (for example, Moshman & Geil, 1998; Sorsana & Troadec, 2007; Troadec & Martinot, 2003) in the social psychology of cognitive development, such a debate invites specification of the role played by all the mediations that are involved in cognitive constructions and that produce systems of interaction with differentiated socio-cognitive dynamics. These include the partners with their roles, their status, their beliefs, their history, their culture; the task with its own architecture and meanings; the context of resolution itself and the contextual parameters of these communicative situations.

The epistemological stake as well as the methodological one is considerable: What is regarded as universal in development? The postulate

Correspondence should be addressed to Christine Sorsana, Université Toulouse II, UFR de Psychologie, Département de Psychologie du Développement, S allées Antonio Machado F-31058 Toulouse, Cedex 9, France. E-mail: sorsana@univ-tlse2.fr

I would like to thank Denis Hilton for comments on English style.

DOI: 10.1080/13546800701851179

T0349528

maintained by cultural psychology consists in thinking that "what is universal—and fundamental for psychological development—is that they are not *the products* of development but rather an *operating mode*, a certain way of engaging formative processes in direct relationship to the social and cultural environment" (Deleau, 2004, p. 16). In other words, a pre-programmed "prêt-à-penser" (readiness-to-think) exists among human babies (Lécuyer, 1991). Admitting the universality of the processes of appropriation of social practices and representations then leads us to "analyse how such processes register the construction of the psychological organization in a social matrix" and to "open also the way to new forms of empirical investigation" (Deleau, 2004, p. 16).

Does interaction constitute *the matrix* of cognition? A "weak" version of this thesis considers interaction as "the solution from which cognition emerges" (Trognon, 1991, p. 20). Interaction would be a catalyst or rather a mediator between the individual and the knowledge to be acquired or interiorized. A "strong" version supposes that "the emergence of cognition is accomplished through *the unfolding* of interaction" (Trognon, 1991, p. 20). Two ways of interpreting the role played by the unfolding of interaction are also possible: (1) *the unfolding* of the interaction plays its role *statically*: such an interpretation is related to studies where the interaction is perceived as (a) "a container of the processes of thought" of participants; or (b) providing "matter to these processes of thought" or (c) offering "models of these processes, which are internalized by the subject"; and (2) *the unfolding* of the interaction plays its role *dynamically* when the researcher considers that the partners co-produce their cognitions: either the partners help each other to "give birth to" a cognition specific to him-or herself; or they fully co-produce new cognitions in the sense that these are irreducible to the sum of their individual cognitions (Trognon, 1991).

Answering these critical questions comes up against a major problem: that of the choice of methods. Many are the researchers who today claim the inadequacy of quantitative methods alone to account for the processes of change, and for inter- and intra-individual dynamics at work in cognitive training (see, notably, Bastien, 1994; Bruner, 1990; Rogoff & Angelillo, 2002; Shotter, 1990; Siegler & Crowley, 1991; Van der Veer & Valsiner, 1991; Verba, 1999). In addition, as noted by Bruner (1990), the study of human mind is so deeply embedded in the dilemma of being both the object and the agent of one's own study, that it cannot limit its approach to using ways of thinking borrowed from physics. What therefore are the alternatives?

Some researchers consider that it would be necessary to question the same problems with different methods that introduce little "interpretative screens between the researcher and his object of study" (Richelle, 1993, p. 222; see also Sorsana & Troadec, 2007). For others, "reasoned methodological conceptualizations" are to be created (Bastien, 1994), by giving priority to a project of metamethodology in order to invent new methodological frameworks, which would be adapted to the modelling of the functioning of complex systems, such as the human cognitive system. In view of such questions, it is clear that today an inversion in the way of formulating psychological questions is occurring, as Richelle (1993) considered it.[1] Taking over for themselves the microgenetic analysis initially developed by Inhelder and her collaborators (see Inhelder et al., 1992; Morgado & Parrat-Dayan, 2002), at the present time, researchers make descriptions as close as possible to "reality" that in return call into question the theoretical discourse. This yields a psychology of "portraits" (Flavell, 1992): that is, very detailed observations of children, for a given period, as well as meticulous and intensive protocol analyses, in order to grasp the complex emergence of cognitive acquisitions, an approach which can be qualified as a "clinical analysis" of rationality (Trognon & Rétornaz, 1989; see also Bastien, 1997; Bernicot, Caron-Pargue, & Trognon, 1997; Bernicot, Trognon, Guidetti, & Musiol, 2002; Bideaud, 1988; Gilly, Roux, & Trognon, 1999; Siegler, 1983).

The contributions of this Special Issue are in keeping with these concerns regarding more adequate methods to describe and analyse, within a same functional unit, at least three levels of comprehension of socio-cognitive phenomena, in relation to *the constraints of the task*: the individual's *cognitive functioning*; the *socio-cognitive functioning* of the dyad or the small group; and, finally, the way the first two elements are mediated by *discursive activities*.

Christine Sorsana's paper introduces this Special Issue by raising several theoretical and methodological questions relating to the analysis of interactions between peers, in problem-solving situations. The various types of socio-discursive analyses currently used in this field of research are pointed out and the author stresses the usefulness of developing an interlocutory analysis of conversational exchanges. She argues that the pragmatic analysis of learning situations is necessary in order to widen our comprehension of cognitive functioning that is embedded in a fully socio-cognitive activity. Some lines of investigation related to the characteristics of dissension that produce *versus* do not produce fresh mutual knowledge are then proposed; in line with these suggestions, a logico-discursive illustration will be presented thereafter by Alain Trognon, Christine Sorsana, Martine Batt and Dominique Longin.

---

[1]"In the dialectical movement specific to science, where, in alternation, the theoretical discourse organizes reality and reality questions and disturbs the theoretical discourse, the next twenty years of psychology will be in this second phase, or will petrify itself in vain scholastics" (Richelle, 1993, p. 222).

The four following articles present empirical evidence of socio-cognitive dynamics within dyads or small groups of children who are working together. Each study is concerned with choosing the methodological tools that are most suitable for a meticulous socio-cognitive analysis. More precisely, the common concern of all the contributors is to situate their respective studies in a research process that consists in going back and forth between theoretical discourse and particular case-based analysis in order to generate new hypotheses arising from the exploration of individual and inter-individual variations. Two methods—which could be complementary in the near future—are selected here. The articles by Valérie Tartas and Anne-Nelly Perret-Clermont and by Isabelle Olry-Louis and Isabelle Soidet both privilege *a systematic coding of behaviours and speech from preset categories*. They develop a pluralistic perspective of interaction that incorporates several levels of analysis. Jean-Paul Roux's article introduces general principles of *a logical analysis of interlocution* the formalization of which is proposed in the paper by Alain Trognon and his colleagues.

Valérie Tartas and Anne-Nelly Perret-Clermont present a qualitative case-based analysis of four dyads with contrasting levels of performance, from a sample of 9- to 10-year-old children who had to solve Kohs cubes problems. Competent-by-instruction children or (spontaneous)-competent children are interacting with novice ones. Dyadic sessions are analysed from the following dimensions related to previous research done by Liengme Bessire, Grossen, Iannaccone and Perret-Clermont (1994) and Nihlohlm and Säljö (1996): (1) making strategies explicit; (2) children's task management; and (3) modes of interaction and their evolution—in order to show that the same collective work instruction will lead to very different socio-cognitive dynamics from one dyad to another. These authors try to situate their method of qualitative analysis from preset categories in a sequential approach to the modes of socio-cognitive management of the task.

Isabelle Olry-Louis and Isabelle Soidet study collaborative learning through texts, presented to pupils from secondary schools. The task consists in writing a synthesis of a documentary file on the topic "*Venice, its current problems, its future prospects*". The authors analyse the forms of co-operation in six peer groups (with 4 children each) on the basis of linguistic indicators, in order to identify the most productive ones, from the point of view of future acquisitions. They consider several levels: that of the collaborative devices—complete *versus* partial, that of the working groups and that of the participants. The various methods of analysing co-operative interactions currently used are noted, i.e., (1) objective methods, (2) interpretative methods, and (3) logical analysis methods. Some of the advantages and the limits of these various tools are specified. Without denying the contribution of sequential methods, the authors justify the reasons why they choose in this study the systematic coding of the linguistic behaviours, in order to try to describe the trilogs and polylogs. More precisely, they carry out an evaluation of the pupils' productions from the standpoint of argumentation, present a questionnaire to evaluate acquisitions on the topic as well as perform an analysis of how the participants operate according to the type of collaboration (complete collaboration—children talk together and produce a collective synthesis *versus* partial collaboration—children talk together and produce an individual synthesis), using two coding grids, from Chabrol and Bromberg (1999) and from Olry-Louis and Soidet (2003), respectively.

Jean-Paul Roux briefly presents general principles from which it is possible to conceive a logical analysis of conversational exchanges allowing us to describe how cognitions occur in conversation. He points out some theoretical and methodological problems encountered in interaction analysis with young children. An illustration of such an analysis is given by Alain Trognon, Christine Sorsana, Martine Batt and Dominique Longin. Using the interlocutory logic, which is a theory of dialogue movement in context, they present a logical-discursive analysis of a process of joint decision making within a dyad, which comes from a sample of children aged 6 to 8 solving the Tower of Hanoi problem. The authors want to show how interlocutory logic can formalize the socio-cognitive conflict, which is an essential "ingredient" for the social psychology of cognitive development.

To the question "What does the subject rely on to solve a task?", the contributors of this Special Issue answer that he/she uses others' support in the first place as a "prop" for his/her own productive capacities. As Beaudichon (1990, p. 196) also emphasizes it, "the concept of an individual who manages by his/her own, from start to finish, all the elements necessary to the execution of the current activity is as abstract as the concept of the epistemic subject. Faced with a problem, what the subject-child is activating in the first place, are also and often procedures of requests for assistance, of requests for confirmation. Among knowledge which is first constituted, the two following 'principles' appear prominent: when one cannot do something by him/herself it is necessary to call somebody who is able to do it; (and) it is more pleasant to do something with somebody else than alone". We hope that the work presented in this Special Issue will help research move beyond the dichotomy that is still present, according to which researchers who "do social analysis" are not fully considered as "cognitivists" (cf. Beaudichon, 1990), by proposing some ways to integrate, in equal measure, the two types of approach.

REFERENCES

Barrouillet, P. (2007). Le raisonnement chez l'enfant et l'adolescent. In S. Rossi & J. B. Van der Henst (Eds.), *Psychologies du raisonnement* (pp. 111–141). Bruxelles, Belgium: De Boeck Université.

Bastien, C. (1994). La recherche sur le raisonnement chez l'enfant. *Psychologie Française, 39*(2), 205–212.

Bastien, C. (1997). *Les connaissances de l'enfant à l'adulte.* Paris: A. Colin.

Beaudichon, J. (1990). En quoi les recherches sur le développement des compétences sociales questionnent-elles les théories générales du développement cognitif? In G. Netchine Grynberg (Ed.), *Développement et fonctionnements cognitifs chez l'enfant: des modèles généraux aux modèles locaux* (pp. 185–199). Paris: Presses Universitaires de France.

Bernicot, J., Caron-Pargue, J., & Trognon, A. (Eds.). (1997). *Conversation, interaction et fonctionnement cognitif.* Nancy, France: Presses Universitaires de Nancy.

Bernicot, J., Trognon, A., Guidetti, M., & Musiol, M. (Eds.). (2002). *Pragmatique et psychologie.* Nancy, France: Presses Universitaires de Nancy.

Bideaud, J. (1988). *Logique et bricolage chez l'enfant.* Lille, France: Presses Universitaires de Lille.

Blaye, A., & Lemaire, P. (Eds.). (2007). *Psychologie du développement cognitif de l'enfant.* Bruxelles, Belgium: De Boeck Université.

Bruner, J. (1990). *Acts of meaning.* Cambridge, MA: Harvard University Press.

Chabrol, C., & Bromberg, M. (1999). Préalables à une classification des actes de parole. *Psychologie française, 44,* 291–306.

Deleau, M. (2004). Le développement psychologique d'un point de vue historico-culturel: enjeux et perspectives. *Bulletin de psychologie, 57*(1), 469, 13–20.

Flavell, J. H. (1992). Cognitive development: Past, present and future. *Developmental Psychology, 28,* 998–1005.

Gilly, M. (1995). Approches socioconstructives du développement cognitif. In G. Gaonach & C. Golder (Eds.), *Manuel de psychologie pour l'enseignement* (pp. 130–167). Paris: Hachette.

Gilly, M., Roux, J. P., & Trognon, A. (Eds.). (1999). *Apprendre dans l'interaction. Analyse des médiations sémiotiques.* Aix-en-Provence & Nancy, France: Publications de l'Université de Provence & Presses Universitaires de Nancy.

Hinde, R. A., Perret-Clermont, A. N., & Stevenson-Hinde, J. (Eds.). (1985). *Social relationships and cognitive development.* Oxford, UK: Clarendon Press.

Inhelder, B., Cellérier, G., Ackermann, E., Blanchet, A., De Caprona, D., Ducret, J. J., et al. (1992). *Le cheminement des découvertes de l'enfant.* Neuchâtel, Switzerland: Delachaux & Niestlé.

Lave, J. (1992). Word problems: A microcosm of theories of learning. In P. Light & G. Butterworth (Eds.), *Context and cognition. Ways of learning and knowing* (pp. 74–91). New York & London: Harvester Wheatsheaf.

Lécuyer, R. (1991). L'intelligence des bébés. *La Recherche, 236*(22), 1158–1165.

Liengme Bessire, M.-J., Grossen, M., Iannaccone, A., & Perret-Clermont, A.-N. (1994). Social comparison of expertise: Interactional patterns and dynamics of instruction. In H. C. Foot, C. J. Howe, A. K. Tolmie, & D. A. E. Warden (Eds.), *Group and interactive learning* (pp. 471–476). Southampton Boston: Computational Mechanics Publishers.

Light, P., & Butterworth, G. (Eds.). (1992). *Context and cognition. Ways of learning and knowing.* New York & London: Harvester Wheatsheaf.

Markovits, H., & Barrouillet, P. (Eds.). (2004). Development and reasoning [Special issue]. *Thinking & Reasoning, 10*(2).

Morgado, L., & Parrat-Dayan, S. (2002). Conversations libres avec l'enfant: problèmes et méthodes. *Bulletin de Psychologie, 55*(6), 462, 645–657.

Moshman, D., & Geil, M. (1998). Collaborative reasoning: Evidence for collective rationality. *Thinking & Reasoning, 4*, 231–248.

Nilholm, C., & Säljö, R. (1996). Co-action, situation definitions and socio-cultural experience. A study of problem solving in mother–child interaction. *Learning and Instruction, 6*(4), 325–344.

Olry-Louis, I., & Soidet, I. (2003). Co-opérer pour co-construire des savoirs: une approche différentielle. *L'Orientation Scolaire et Professionnelle, 32*, 503–535.

Perret-Clermont, A. N., & Nicolet, M. (Eds.). (2001). *Interagir et connaître: Enjeux et régulations sociales dans le développement cognitif.* Paris: L'Harmattan. (First edition, 1988).

Politzer, G. (Ed.). (2002). *Le raisonnement humain.* Paris: Hermès.

Richelle, M. (1993). *Du nouveau sur l'esprit?* Paris: Presses Universitaires de France.

Rogoff, B., & Angelillo, C. (2002). Investigating the co-ordinated functioning of multifaceted cultural practices in human development. *Human Development, 45*, 211–225.

Schliemann, A. D., Carraher, D. W., & Ceci, S. J. (1997). Everyday cognition. In J. W. Berry, P. R. Dasen, & T. S. Saraswathi (Eds.), *Handbook of cross-cultural psychology. Vol. 2: Basic processes and human development* (pp. 177–216). Boston: Allyn & Bacon.

Shotter, J. (1990). Getting in touch: The metamethodology of a postmodern science of mental life. In J. Shotter (Ed.), *Knowing of the third kind* (pp. 35–46). Utrecht, Belgium: ISOR, University of Utrecht.

Siegler, R. S. (1983). Information processing approaches to development. In P. H. Mussen & W. Kessen (Eds.), *Handbook of child psychology. Vol. 1: History, theory and methods* (pp. 129–211). New York: Wiley.

Siegler, R. S. (1998). *Children's thinking* Hillsdale, NJ: Prentice Hall (First edition, 1986).

Siegler, R. S., & Crowley, K. (1991). The microgenetic method: A direct means for studying cognitive development? *American Psychologist, 46*, 606–620.

Sorsana, C. (1999). *Psychologie des interactions sociocognitives.* Paris: A. Colin (collection Synthèse).

Sorsana, C. (2001). Dynamiques sociales et cognitives des acquisitions. In C. Golder & D. Gaonach (Eds.), *Enseigner à des adolescents. manuel de psychologie* (pp. 208–233). Paris: Hachette (Education).

Sorsana, C., & Troadec, B. (2007). Facteurs socioculturels et développement cognitif. In A. Blaye & P. Lemaire (Eds.), *Le développement cognitif de l'enfant* (pp. 283–312). Bruxelles, Belgium: De Boeck Université.

Troadec, B., & Martinot, C. (2003). *Le développement cognitif. Théories actuelles de la pensée en contextes.* Paris: Belin.

Trognon, A. (1991). L'interaction en général: sujets, groupes, cognitions, représentations sociales. *Connexions, 57*(1), 9–25.

Trognon, A., & Rétornaz, A. (1989). Clinique du rationnel: psychologie cognitive et analyse des conversations. *Connexions, 57*(1), 9–25.

Van der Veer, R., & Valsiner, J. (1991). *Understanding Vygotski. A quest for synthesis.* Oxford, UK: Blackwell.

Verba, M. (1999). L'analyse des dynamiques interactives dans la construction des savoirs chez les jeunes enfants. In M. Gilly, J. P. Roux, & A. Trognon (Eds.), *Apprendre dans l'interaction. Analyse des médiations sémiotiques* (pp. 181–200). Aix-en-Provence & Nancy, France: Presses de l'Université de Provence & Presses Universitaires de Nancy.

EUROPEAN JOURNAL OF DEVELOPMENTAL PSYCHOLOGY
2008, 5 (5), 544–560

Peer's verbal interactions specificity on cognitive development

Christine Sorsana

University of Toulouse 2, Toulouse, and University of Nancy 2, Nancy, France

In the field of cognitive development, the specificity of symmetrical interactions (child/child) is of interest because such an interaction, based on equality between participants (as opposed to adult/child interaction), is assumed to give rise to co-operation (Piaget, 1932; Youniss, 1980). Co-operative interaction is supposed to introduce a functional interdependence because it promotes a motivation to be, and act, with others. But it also encourages the search for agreement on ideas and intentions, and the finding of a good solution for both participants. Nevertheless, a child's goal is not always to co-operate and peer interaction has multiple meanings (Grossen, 1994). In other respects, interaction with an (expert) adult seems to remain necessary in order to construct epistemic knowledge (Baker, Leoni, & Perret-Clermont, 1978). Thus, the consideration of interlocutory characteristics of children's exchanges is proposed. Specifically those characteristics that are likely to allow, or not allow, individual cognitive benefits. More precisely, we will discuss the characteristics of "transactive or exploratory" discourse, which is assumed to produce fresh knowledge because "the child is committed in a critical and constructive way to work on the partner's reasoning" (Bachmann, 2001, p. 2; Mercer, 1995, 2000; Teasley, 1995; Wegerif, Mercer, & Rojas-Drummond, 1999).

Keywords: Cognitive development; Social interaction; Conversation; Interlocutory analysis; Peer interaction.

Correspondence should be addressed to Christine Sorsana, Université Toulouse II, UFR de Psychologie, Département de psychologie du développement, 5 allées Antonio Machado, F-31058 Toulouse Cedex 9, France. E-mail: sorsana@univ-tlse2.fr

This article is based on a presentation given at the symposium "Dynamics of interlocution and cognitive development", XIth European Conference on Developmental Psychology, Mailand, Italy, 27–31 August 2003.

Author's note: I would like to thank Ciarán O'Keeffe for comments on English style.

http://www.psypress.com/edp   DOI: 10.1080/17405620701859159

Our objective here is twofold. First, we want to recall some empirical studies that consider the verbal characteristics of children's exchanges that are likely to allow (or not) individual cognitive benefits. Then, we raise and put in debate some theoretical and methodological questions that remain unanswered.

THEORETICAL MODELS DESCRIBING THE IMPACT OF SOCIAL FACTORS ON COGNITIVE DEVELOPMENT

The theoretical models that proposed a description of social factors relating to child's cognitive development initially took the asymmetrical child/adult configuration and focused on the analysis of guidance situations. Among these models, the notion of imitation is considered as the primary socio-cognitive process from an ontogenetic point of view. This is in reference to the parent (mother)/child "primary dyad", which constitutes the base of the interactive system of knowledge acquisition and transmission (cf. Bruner, 1983; Deleau, 1990; Pêcheux, 1995; Wertsch, 1985; Winnykamen, 1990). Thereafter, the child diversifies his tools of acquisition; the imitative process would remain a privileged modality "when it only makes it possible to reduce uncertainty as to the value of the behaviour" (Winnykamen, 1990, p. 326).

Interest relating to the specificity of symmetrical relationships (child/child) for the construction of knowledge has since been increasing. Such interest has relied on the premise that these kinds of relationships, founded on equality between partners (as opposed to adult/child interactions), will generate co-operation (Piaget, 1932; Youniss, 1980). In other words, there is a similar cognitive, social and emotional maturity between peers. There is no authority, no knowledge or cognitive skill imposed from the beginning of the interaction, but everything is negotiated between them. As Youniss (1980) said, "Self is not inferior to other in knowledge or power but self and other are equals in the right to understand and the power to construct knowledge. Unlike the system which children believe adults already know, the one created by collaborating peers has no definite endpoint. It is open to redefinition through a democratic process founded in methods of reciprocity" (p. 19).

In line with this, many researchers (cf. Hartup, 1985; Krappmann, 1985) posit that the middle of infancy is a particularly sensitive period for the structuring of peer relationships which has long-term developmental implications for interaction and cognitive abilities.

Co-operation between peers—described in particular by Piaget (1932) as "a source of thought and self-awareness", dissociating "subjective attitude from an objective one", and a "source of regulation"—is acknowledged in many studies that demonstrate the cognitive benefits of social interactions in the development of knowledge (see Gilly, 1995; Sorsana, 1999a, 2001, 2003). An experimenter asks children to solve a task together and he/she expects that they will co-operate. Furthermore, co-operation is the underlying hypothesis that explains the individual cognitive progress observed between children who worked together compared to observed performances of children who worked alone, as studied in the research discipline known as Socio-Cognitive Conflict. Such progress is defined as a co-operative interaction between two (or three) individuals led to give *conflicting answers* in a verbal and/or gestural mode but who are so cognitively engaged in the task that they easily overcome this social and cognitive disruption. This is regardless of the study perspective, whether a structural perspective (Doise & Mugny, 1997; Doise, Mugny, & Perret-Clermont, 1975; Mugny, 1991; Perret-Clermont, 1996) or a procedural one (Gilly, 1991, 1993, 1995). However, these theoretical conjectures probably mask another reality: perhaps the children's aim is not always to co-operate.

THEORETICAL AND METHODOLOGICAL QUESTIONS IN PEER INTERACTIONS IN PROBLEM-SOLVING SITUATIONS

In the light of studies based on adult/child interactions in testing situations, Grossen (1994) raised four theoretical and methodological questions for peer interactions.

Polysemous nature of interactions between peers in problem-solving situations

When an experimenter asks children to solve a task together, he/she expects that children will co-operate. But what is the nature of the activity to be carried out from the children's point of view? Is their goal really to co-operate? In reality, given the presence of an experimenter (although always an observer, he/she is never considered a confounding factor) such situations have multiple meanings (Grossen, 1994):

- Socio-cognitive and emotional processes are involved: level of children's expertise; presence of struggle for leadership; domination or co-operation; potential feelings of failure or prestige about others; desire to make a good impression, etc.
- Various goals are pursued: to undertake the task as a challenge or obligation or to show own skills; to want to play; to dissimulate own ignorance or to look like a co-operative person in front of an unknown experimenter; to want to help, etc.

Links between micro-, meso- and macro-contexts in the study of peer interactions

What are the favoured macro- and meso-elements when the researcher is interpreting observed events from a micro-context? On the one hand, some elements of the relational, social and institutional children's experiment are transposed, used and interpreted to find some meaning of this new problem-solving context. In addition, the partners' social positions are elicited in order to be negotiated and interpreted another time in the conversation. The question then becomes how can such interactional dynamics be measured? On the other hand, the question is how to divide the interaction analysis into space and time units?

Experimental staging of interactive situations between children

Which types of interactions are induced by an experimental setting "A" compared to setting "B"? Grossen (1994) emphasizes how it is necessary to consider experimental settings as more than tools for observing behaviours. The setting is then also empirical data. Moreover, the impact of the experimenter's presence must be taken into account in the analyses of the particular socio-cognitive phenomena under examination (Grossen, Liengme Bessire, & Perret-Clermont, 1997).

The nature of the information collected in interactive situations between children

We know that the social circumstance of the children's situation interferes directly with their constructed meaning of it. Related to this, interactions between peers, when asymmetry is not caused at the outset, appear to be exclusive situations where it is possible to understand the meaning the child forms gradually about the task. This kind of under-standing is not easily available in face-to-face adult/child situations, because, ultimately, there is a relationship based on authority and power due to the adult's presence.

In addition to all the previous questions raised by Grossen (1994) we propose that *each situation observed takes place within a conversational setting* (Sorsana, 1999a, 1999b, 2003, 2005; Sorsana & Musiol, 2005). Participants use language to answer an adult speaker, or other partners, in order to manage the different stages of the task resolution. Moreover, most of the recent explanations about the effectiveness of dyadic interaction stress the importance of communicative exchanges that appear in joint problem-solving situations (Ellis & Gauvain, 1992; Garton & Pratt, 2001).

RECALL OF THE TYPES OF LANGUAGE ANALYSES FOCUSED ON PROBLEM-SOLVING SITUATIONS

As observed by Teasley (1995), the idea that verbalization can affect a problem's resolution is not a new idea in psychology. Two different types of studies suggest that the co-ordination of thoughts can have an effect on the content of what it is learned: studies of "private" (or egocentric) speech and "thinking aloud" studies.

Private-speech studies

Work relating to the study of egocentric speech, which children produce spontaneously in their everyday activities, suggests that "private" speech has a positive impact on problem solving. This is because it provides various functions of self-regulation, such as increasing attention focus, identifying distinctive task features, planning solutions and guiding motor activity (Diaz, 1992; Vergnaud, 1991). A review by Berk (1992) reported studies in which the amount of task-relevant private speech was associated with successful problem solving, even if such positive effects were not always immediately salient. These studies, however, provide few precise conclusions concerning the link between linguistic content and performance. As mentioned by Teasley (1995), because the egocentric speech is supposed to support self-regulation, coding utterances do not relate specifically to the actual content. For example, utterances such as word game or repetition have been coded as *self-stimulatory* (Kohlberg, Yeager, & Hjertholm, 1968) and statements describing ongoing activity have been coded as *focusing activity* (Balamore & Wozniak, 1984). This type of coding describes what speech could accomplish, but it doesn't differentiate between the various types of utterances and their relationship with the problem resolution. For example, *self-stimulatory* can serve a goal of motivation while *focusing activity* can contribute to the identification of critical task components. Thus, these two functions can be considered as self-regulatory but they ultimately involve different aspects of the cognitive process. The analysis of the verbal activity used in such studies does not make it possible to examine the role of the specific kind of egocentric speech used in problem solving (Teasley, 1995).

In summary, the production of private speech (or egocentric speech) is positively related to performance when children are working alone. "As the correlations were generally between frequency of egocentric speech and performance, the assumption is that more speech leads to more learning. What is not clear from this work is whether particular types of talk might be more important than others" (Teasley, 1995, p. 208).

Think-aloud studies

In cognitive psychology, researchers have specifically wondered about the validity of the think-aloud methodology. Analyses have focused on the presence or absence of verbalization rather than on the content of the verbalization and have led to the conclusion that the amount of talk is what matters, like in private-speech studies. However, when verbalization was present and analysed, results have shown that speech can improve problem solving when "that talk consists of articulating information that is not normally considered, such as reasons or motives (e.g., Ahlum-Heath & Di Vesta, 1986; Berry, 1990; Berry & Broadbent, 1984; Gagne & Smith, 1962). This type of verbalization is assumed to improve performance because it requires interpretative processing, which relates information in the individual's short-term memory to thoughts or information attended to previously (Ericsson & Simon, 1984)" (Teasley, 1995, p. 208).

Comparison between verbal protocols of good problem solvers *versus* poor problem solvers provides support for the idea that verbalization helps to the extent that it provokes an interpretative process. Teasley (1995, p. 208) stated that "good problem solvers are more likely than poor problem solvers to state rules for their actions (before or after the actions are taken) and spontaneously make evaluative statements (Gick & Holyoak, 1980; Thorndyke & Stasz, 1980)". In addition, good problem solvers generated more explanations and comprehension monitoring statements than the poor problem solvers (Chi, Bassok, Lewis, Reimann, & Glaser, 1989; Chi, de Leeuw, Chiu, & LaVancher, 1994, quoted in Teasley, 1995). The amount of talk (as measured by protocol lines) did not differ between good and poor problem solvers. Researchers, therefore, assumed that the content of subjects' talk (in these cases, students) was responsible for the significant differences in performance and concluded that the benefits of verbalization came from the articulation of inferences that called on students to integrate their knowledge.

In summary, work in information processing provides strong evidence that verbalization is related to learning. Teasley (1995) stated, "furthermore, it is not the simple production of talk that improves problem solving, but rather that the internal processing can be changed by the verbalization. Specifically, studies using think-aloud procedures have found significant correlations between talk that consists of interpretations—such as explanations, justifications, rules, or principles—and learning" (p. 208).

Talk produced by interacting partners

Another type of verbal analyses concerns talk produced between interacting partners. Successful dyads (Gilly & Deblieux, 1999; Teasley, 1995):

- give more explanations (cf. Gilly & Deblieux, 1999; Swing & Peterson, 1982; Webb, 1982);
- engage in more sophisticated argumentation, clarification and negotiation (cf. Berkowitz & Gibbs, 1983; Eisenberg & Garvey, 1981; Gilly & Deblieux, 1999; Kruger & Tomasello, 1986; Leadbeater, 1988); and
- participate in more discussions of plans, goals and strategies (cf. Cooper, 1980; Forman & Cazden, 1985; Glachan & Light, 1982; Perlmutter, Behrend, Kuo, & Muller, 1989).

As observed by Teasley (1995), it seems likely that successful collaborations include the specific types of verbalization that have also been shown by think-aloud studies to improve performance.

SOME UNANSWERED QUESTIONS

Among the unanswered questions relating to the previous studies, the following are worthy of mention:

- Can a specific type of relationship between participants involve a specific type of strategy to solve a problem?
- Which "configurations" of interaction (or which ways of communicating) are most efficient in coping with the cognitive constraints of a specific task? It is important to relate the processes of communication to the outcomes of joint activity.
- Is it possible to identify some efficient interlocutory "structures" whatever the kind of dialogical context?
- What are the interlocutory characteristics of disagreements that produce original knowledge?

Some "hints" of possible answers come from various studies that compared: verbalization *versus* no-verbalization conditions and dyadic *versus* lone work conditions. These were conducted using decision-making problems (Fletcher, 1985, quoted by Teasley, 1995) or using concept-attainment problems (Durling & Shick, 1976, quoted by Teasley, 1995). Additionally, studies compared verbalization-alone conditions *versus* silent-alone conditions *versus* verbalizing dyads (Durling & Shick, 1976) or verbalizing triads (Fletcher, 1985). The results ordered into effective experimental conditions are as follows: verbalizing dyads performed better than verbalization-alone-condition dyads, which performed better than silent-condition dyads, which performed better than no-verbalizing dyads (Durling & Shick, 1976). This is noted by Teasley (1995), "... both studies concluded that verbalization was a more powerful predictor of performance than the group *versus* individual variable. However, the role of verbalization in collaboration remains unclear. Because these studies did not characterize the talk produced in the verbalizing conditions, it is not known whether dyads and alones produced the same kind of talk, or why talk might have had an effect in either condition" (p. 209).

In Teasley's (1995) study, 70 children (aged 8 to 11) were assigned to work on a scientific reasoning task either alone or with a partner. Within these two conditions, half of the children were allowed or encouraged to talk, and the other half were asked not to talk. The results ordered into effective experimental conditions are as follows: talk dyads performed better than no-talk alones, which were almost the same as the talk alone condition. Finally, no-talk dyads performed the worst.

The main results show the talk dyad condition was superior compared to children—with partners or alone—who did not talk. Analyses of the children's activity with the task, as measured by quantity and quality of experiments, showed no significant difference between experimental groups. Such results suggest that the effects of talk were not attributable to different experiences with the task (Teasley, 1995). The major difference between hypotheses produced by talk-alone *versus* talk-dyad conditions is based on the speed with which dyads developed correct and more elaborate hypotheses. However, the talk condition did not produce significantly better quality hypotheses for children working alone. In addition, the rate at which an overall hypothesis was generated was actually quicker for no-talk alones than for talk alones. In contrast, talk was clearly beneficial for dyads. But, as in the previous study by Durling and Shick (1976), Teasley (1995) also found a performance considerably worse for the no-talk dyads.

To explain the peer collaboration superiority, Teasley (1995) suggested that collaboration leads to learning not because of the collaboration per se, but rather because the collaboration increases the likelihood that children engage themselves in forms of interpretative talk. The question is essentially, why are two heads better than one? It is undoubtedly because such a communicative setting contains an implicit *obligation* to co-ordinate conversational coherence (Grice, 1989) to maintain the ongoing task activity. Recognition of this obligation develops early in life (Keenan, 1983) and is evident by middle childhood (Cooper, Marquis, & Edwards, 1986). In other words, "to manage coherence and activity simultaneously, partners must make utterances that signal intentions, current interpretations, and expectations. Within the context of a shared problem-solving task, these utterances take the form of plans, strategies, and explanations" (Teasley, 1995, p. 218), such as those found in think-aloud studies and private-speech studies. Moreover, the fact of merely anticipating a context of interaction with a partner led to cognitive benefits when subjects were working alone (Cohen, 1961; Davis, Stasser, Spitzer, & Holt, 1976; Tetlock,

1983; Zajonc, 1960). Such results are similarly found with children (Doise, Rijsman, Van Meel, Bressers, & Pinxten, 1981). Supporting this data, Teasley (1995) claimed that the performance of children working alone could be due to the fact that they were more aware that they would be heard by the experimenter, so they maintained a social obligation to be coherent and explicit. According to Teasley (1995), "if this assumption is correct, then any procedure that reproduces the social obligation for coherence that is implicit in language should result in interpretive thinking without actual vocalization or the presence of a partner" (p. 218).

To summarize, there are four major assumptions related to dyadic efficiency in problem-solving situations:

- learning is facilitated by exposure to a greater number and diversity of explanations and possible solutions (cf. Azmitia, 1988; Zimmerman & Blom, 1983);
- dyadic activity can produce a socio-cognitive conflict due to exposure to others' ideas (cf. Doise & Mugny, 1997; Doise et al., 1975; Mugny, 1991; Perret-Clermont, 1996);
- dyadic communication has specificities, such as co-construction (cf. Damon & Phelps, 1989) and intersubjectivity (Forman, 1992; Grossen, 1988). These studies have stressed the importance of input from both partners; and
- such a communication setting incorporates a social obligation to co-ordinate conversational coherence and to explicit intentions, interpretations and expectations to maintain the ongoing activity (Teasley, 1995).

THE INTERLOCUTORY ANALYSIS PERSPECTIVE

The currently available description of exchanges that produce fresh knowledge remains rough. Researchers agree that they comprise utterances of: actions planning goals and strategies; explanations and justifications; argumentations; clarifications; sophisticated negotiations and evaluative statements. For example, Mercer (2000) claimed there are three types of verbal exchanges that articulate thoughts of oneself and others: "Using language, we can link our intellects together in a variety of ways. We may build the uncritical, non-competitive and constructive relationship of *cumulative talk*', in which individual differences of perception or judgement are minimized. We may treat our talk partners as a threat (menace) to the pursuit of our individual interests, in *disputational talk*', in which the participants work to keep their identities separate, and to protect their individuality. Or we may engage in a dialogue in which differences are treated explicitly, as matters for mutual exploration, reasoned evaluation and resolution, which I have called '*exploratory talk*'. Exploratory talk, with its explicit reasons, criticisms and evaluations, is a model of dialogue in which participants are not primarily concerned with protecting their separate identities and interests, but instead with ways of jointly and rationally making sense. The notion of exploratory talk captures an ideal—a discussion in which all participants are striving, in a committed but unselfish manner, to establish the best solution. Each participant can make a creative contribution to the sense making and the most useful interpretation may be arrived at eventually through a discussion of the various individual interpretations offered. Of course, these models of talk are simplifications of complex reality which will need to be refined, or even replaced, as we learn more about the nature of interthinking" (Mercer, 2000, p. 173).

A great methodological problem then arises. The problem is the capturing, in a precise way, of utterances as a *joint activity* of the two speakers, whatever their roles and status. Before the transmission of information related to problem solving both partners have to build the "rules of the game" of their verbal exchange, to define the stakes as well as their respective roles and to negotiate their common topic (Caron, 1983; Ghiglione & Trognon, 1993). Thus, *it is a fully socio-cognitive activity*. Consequently, we must insist on the pragmatic dimension of the learning situations, which does not appear in previously reported studies, in order to widen our comprehension of cognitive functioning. To analyse this dimension, the field of pragmatics—the study of the use of language—today provides a theoretical and methodological framework to analyse cognitive processes attained in verbal exchanges (Bernicot, Caron-Pargue, & Trognon, 1997; Bernicot, & Trognon, 2002). More precisely, this discipline aims to describe and explain, using non-linguistic principles, processes of inference that the partners in conversation have implemented to reach the meaning of statements. It is supported by the idea according to which "our linguistic behaviours are ordered by rules or universal rational principles" (Musiol, 1996, p. 49).

Taking into account the analysis of language use in problem-solving situations, there are several points of interest:

- in contrast with the formal analysis of language, the study of its use is an extra-linguistic treatment that allows the articulation of social and cognitive variables *via* conceptual tools such as "communication" and "representation" (cf. Bernicot et al., 1997; Bernicot, Trognon, Guidetti, & Musiol, 2002; Gilly, Roux, & Trognon, 1999; Perret-Clermont, Schubauer-Leoni, & Trognon, 1992); and
- pragmatic analysis is going to form new empirical data because it allows the analysis of step-by-step unfolding cognitive activity from

TABLE 1

Outline of characteristics of dissension that produce versus do not produce fresh mutual knowledge

Conversational management of disagreements

Producing fresh mutual knowledge	*Not producing fresh mutual knowledge*
• *Implicit disagreement* (different ways of accomplishment): ◇ ask for justifications (with modulation of the degree of power of the request: "Why?", "Why was it more important...?"); ◇ direct expression of disagreement using an expressive attenuator ("Yes... but I do not want to...", "I don't believe that it is important...") or using deontic arguments with explicit reference to the rules of the game, between younger children (and in another context of problem-solving) ("We have not the right", "It is necessary to..."); ◇ symmetrical exchanges, like proposition/proposition where the partner puts his/her proposition next to the partner's proposal.	• *Explicit disagreement*: ◇ Direct formulation ("No", "Oh no", "But no", etc.); ◇ orders; ◇ oppositions between assertions (A: yes/B: no); ◇ interrupting the partner's utterance or the partner's action. • *Absence of basic structure question/answer.* • *Literal meaning* of speech acts is exclusively taken into account. • *Disqualification of the partner* (between young children).

the sequences of actions, and their sequential nature, with the aim of identifying the "trace" of cognitive operations.

For example, previous studies give an initial outline of the conversational management of "productive" disagreements *versus* "non-productive" ones of fresh mutual knowledge acquisition (Sorsana, 2005). This "initial outline" comes from studies focused on socio-cognitive interactions between children, at various ages: aged 4–6 (Guizard, 2001), aged 6–8 (Sorsana, 1996, 1997, 1999b, 2003; Sorsana & Musiol, 2005) and aged 10–11 (Gilly et Deblieux, 1999) (cf. Table 1).

CONCLUSION

It is difficult to overlook the language medium when one finds oneself in a learning or problem-solving situation. Yet a certain derived concept of cognitive development has long maintained the contrast between social and cognitive, for the benefit of studying representation, much to the detriment of communication. Today, some researchers think that such a distinction ceased when an obstacle to the analysis of cognitive functioning was generated, e.g., Caron-Pargue (1997) stated: "the language, and more particularly, the conversation could be a place where the surpassing of this controversy occurs, considering that communication and representation are two inseparable sides of a same entity, that we could, for that matter, cut out some other way" (p. 10).

The position granted to social context in the study of socio-cognitive processes related to the development of knowledge became more and more complex following the initial empirical studies on this topic (beginning with the *psycho-social* approach: see Doise et al., 1975). Consequently, today, researchers are considering that the behavioural characteristics of individuals confronted with cognitive tasks do not reflect operational mechanisms exclusively but rather the interpretative processes involved in exchanges and the characterisation of the socio-relational situation in which the task has to be solved. Such interpretations are always negotiated in a context of "dialogue". Such considerations also abandon a "monadic" approach to human cognitive functioning (i.e., focused solely on the individual). Consequently a new unit of analysis is adopted that remains difficult to circumscribe (Trognon & Sorsana, 2005).

This work, however, conducted in the domain of social psychology of cognitive development, has demonstrated that any social situation is not conducive to the acquisition of knowledge. One may rightfully ask why this is the case. Indeed, if one looks closer, any interpersonal encounter appears to come with "constraints" capable of stimulating the cognitive activity of interacting individuals.

First, several studies have shown that initiating a thesis within an exchange, for example, *actually* establishes an interactional constraint. Indeed, initiating a thesis (an idea, a proposition for action) constrains the speaker to support it, to the best of their ability, until closing *and* to defend it, in real time. As a matter of fact, we noticed, in studied children's *corpora*, that the child who initiates a transaction is most often the one who ends it, by negotiating an idea on a theme (Sorsana & Musiol, 2005). Such reports are also found in situations between adults. The cognitive activity deployed in the interlocution thus appears far more important compared to when the subject works individually or when she/he is interrogated, after the fact, on what she/he has achieved. In other words, the articulated liberty is in reality constrained in the interaction and introduces a cognitive "load". The reasons for this are because the initiator is strongly engaged in the consequences of her/his initial pronouncement since she/he offered a part of her/his thoughts. She/he becomes somehow constrained to make her/his idea reach a conclusion, both because there is internally a motivation specific to the drive of the theme, and a "face" to maintain or to make known, identity stakes, etc. Consequently, in the third round of delivery, she/he must calculate and react to the proximity (or distance) which exists between the goal of her/his initial pronouncement and what her/his interlocutor reconstructs when she/he expresses it herself/himself during the second round (Musiol, 2002). More occurs than simply verbalization when two people talk. The "talking-together" that occurs makes the emergence of differences between choices and interpretations, and the expression of exchanges (clarification, rephrasing), functionally necessary for making a later decision.

Finally, children working in dyads appear better armed to face unsettling questions from adults (experimenters, teachers, etc.) since they can (a) consult together (b) support one another to sustain a decision, and/or (c) resume their discussions and confront their respective ideas in case of doubt: "They have a social space of exchange at their disposal which gives them more power in their relations with the adult and a better control of the social situation they find themselves confronted with" (Gilly & Deblieux, 1999, pp. 100–101).

Given that the constraints inherent to any social encounter should make the cognitive stimulation of partners necessary, the question thus becomes: for what reasons do some social interaction situations not lead to cognitive progress?

REFERENCES

Ahlum-Heath, M. E., & Di Vesta, F. J. (1986). The effect of conscious controlled verbalization of a cognitive strategy on transfer in problem solving. *Memory and Cognition, 14,* 281–285.

Azmitia, M. (1988). Peer interaction and problem solving: When are two heads better than one? *Child Development, 59,* 87–96.

Bachmann, K. (2001). *Etude des explications dans une situation de tutorat entre enfants.* Communication to the International Conference "L'explication: enjeux cognitifs et communicationnels". Université René Descartes, 30 novembre–1er décembre.

Baker, N., Leoni, M. L., & Perret-Clermont, A. N. (1978, June). Fondements psychologiques du travail de groupe en situation pédagogique. *Techniques d'instruction, 2,* 8–11.

Balamore, U., & Wozniak, R. H. (1984). Speech–action co-ordination in young children. *Developmental Psychology, 20,* 850–858.

Berk, L. E. (1992). Children's private speech: An overview of theory and the status of research. In R. M. Diaz & L. E. Berk (Eds.), *Private speech: From social interaction to self-regulation* (pp. 17–53). Hillsdale, NJ: Lawrence Erlbaum Associates, Inc.

Berkowitz, M., & Gibbs, J. (1983). Measuring the developmental features of moral discussion. *Merrill-Palmer Quaterly, 29,* 399–410.

Bernicot, J., Caron-Pargue, J., & Trognon, A. (Eds.). (1997). *Conversation, interaction et fonctionnement cognitif.* Nancy, France: Presses Universitaires de Nancy.

Bernicot, J., & Trognon, A. (2002). Le tournant pragmatique en psychologie. In J. Bernicot, A. Trognon, M. Guidetti, & M. Musiol (Eds.), *Pragmatique et psychologie* (pp. 13–32). Nancy, France: Presses Universitaires de Nancy.

Bernicot, J., Trognon, A., Guidetti, M., & Musiol, M. (2002). *Pragmatique et psychologie.* Nancy, France: Presses Universitaires de Nancy.

Berry, D. C. (1990). Talking about cognitive processes. In K. J. Gilhooly, M. T. G. Keane, R. H. Logie, & G. Erdos (Eds.), *Lines of thinking* (Vol. 2, pp. 87–98). Chichester, UK: Wiley.

Berry, D. C., & Broadbent, D. E. (1984). On the relationship between task performance and associated verbalizable knowledge. *Quarterly Journal of Experimental Psychology, 36,* 209–231.

Bruner, J. S. (1983). *Le développement de l'enfant: savoir faire, savoir dire.* Paris: Presses Universitaires de France.

Caron, J. (1983). *Les régulations du discours.* Paris: Presses Universitaires de France.

Caron-Pargue, J. (1997). Préface. In J. Bernicot, J. Caron-Pargue, & A. Trognon (Eds.), *Conversation, interaction et fonctionnement cognitif.* Nancy, France: Presses Universitaires de Nancy.

Chi, M., Bassok, M., Lewis, M., Reimann, P., & Glaser, R. (1989). Self-explanations: How students study and use examples in learning to solve problems. *Cognitive Science, 13,* 145–182.

Chi, M., de Leeuw, N., Chiu, M., & LaVancher, C. (1994). Eliciting self-explanations improves learning. *Cognitive Science, 18,* 439–477.

Cohen, A. R. (1961). Cognitive tuning a factor affecting impression formation. *Journal of Personality, 29,* 235–245.

Cooper, C. R. (1980). Development of collaborative problem solving among preschool children. *Developmental Psychology, 16,* 433–440.

Cooper, C. R., Marquis, A., & Edwards, D. (1986). Four perspectives on peer learning among elementary school children. In E. C. Mueller & C. R. Cooper (Eds.), *Process and outcome in peer relations* (pp. 269–300). New York: Academic Press.

Damon, W., & Phelps, E. (1989). Critical distinctions among three approaches to peer education. *International Journal of Education Research, 13,* 9–19.

Davis, J. H., Stasser, G., Spitzer, C. E., & Holt, R. W. (1976). Changes in group members' preferences during discussion: An illustration with mock injuries. *Journal of Personality and Social Psychology, 34,* 1177–1187.

Deleau, M. (1990). *Les origines sociales du développement mental: Communication et symboles dans la première enfance.* Paris: A. Colin.

Diaz, R. M. (1992). Methodological concerns in the study of private speech. In R. M. Diaz & L. E. Berk (Eds.), *Private speech: From social interaction to self-regulation* (pp. 55–81). Hillsdale, NJ: Lawrence Erlbaum Associates, Inc.

Doise, W., & Mugny, G. (1997). *Psychologie sociale et développement cognitif.* Paris: A. Colin. (First edition, 1981).

Doise, W., Mugny, G., & Perret-Clermont, A. N. (1975). Social interaction and the development of cognitive operations. *European Journal of Social Psychology, 5,* 367–383.

Doise, W., Rijsman, J., Van Meel, J., Bressers, I., & Pinxten, W. (1981). Sociale marketing en cognitieve ontwikkelling. *Pedagogische Studien, 58,* 241–248.

Durling, R., & Shick, C. (1976). Concept attainment by pairs and individuals as a function of vocalization. *Journal of Educational Psychology, 68,* 83–91.

Eisenberg, A. R., & Garvey, C. (1981). Children's use of verbal strategies in resolving conflicts. *Discourse Processes, 4,* 149–170.

Ellis, S., & Gauvain, M. (1992). Social and cultural influences on children's collaborative interactions. In L. T. Winnegar & J. Valsiner (Eds.), *Children's development within social contexts* (pp. 155–180). Hillsdale, NJ: Lawrence Erlbaum Associates, Inc.

Ericsson, K. A., & Simon, H. A. (1984). *Protocol analysis: Verbal reports as data.* Cambridge, MA: MIT Press.

Fletcher, B. (1985). Group and individual learning of junior school children on a microcomputer-based task: Social or cognitive facilitation? *Educational Review, 37,* 251–261.

Forman, E. A. (1992). Discourse, intersubjectivity and the development of peer collaborations: A Vygotskian approach. In L. T. Winnegar & J. Valsiner (Eds.), *Children's development within social contexts* (pp. 126–154). Hillsdale, NJ: Lawrence Erlbaum Associates, Inc.

Forman, E. A., & Cazden, C. B. (1985). Exploring Vygotskian perspectives in education: The cognitive value of peer interaction. In J. V. Wertsch (Ed.), *Culture, communication and cognition: Vygotskian perspectives* (pp. 323–347). New York: Cambridge University Press.

Gagne, R. M., & Smith, E. C. (1962). A study of the effects of verbalization on problem solving. *Journal of Experimental Psychology, 63,* 12–18.

Garton, A. F., & Pratt, C. (2001). Peer assistance in children's problem solving. *British Journal of Developmental Psychology, 19,* 307–318.

Ghiglione, R., & Trognon, A. (1993). *Où va la pragmatique? De la pragmatique à la psychologie sociale.* Grenoble, France: Presses Universitaires de Grenoble.

Gick, M. L., & Holyoak, K. J. (1980). Analogical problem solving. *Cognitive Psychology, 12,* 306–335.

Gilly, M. (1991). Social psychology of cognitive constructions: European perspectives. In M. Carretero, M. Pope, S. Robertjan, & J. L. Pozo (Eds.), *Learning and instruction. European Research in an international context* (Vol. III, pp. 99–123). Oxford, UK: Pergamon Press.

Gilly, M. (1993). Psychologie sociale des constructions cognitives: Perspectives européennes. *Bulletin de Psychologie, XLVI*(412), 671–683.

Gilly, M. (1995). Approches socioconstructives du développement cognitif. In G. Gaonach, & C. Golder (Eds.), *Manuel de psychologie pour l'enseignement* (pp. 130–167). Paris: Hachette.

Gilly, M., & Deblieux, M. (1999). Analyse des médiations langagières en situation dyadique de résumé de récit. In M. Gilly, J. P. Roux, & A. Trognon (Eds.), *Apprendre dans l'interaction. Analyse des médiations sémiotiques* (pp. 95–120). Aix-en-Provence & Nancy, France: Presses Universitaires de Provence & Presses Universitaires de Nancy.

Gilly, M., Roux, J. P., & Trognon, A. (Eds.). (1999). *Apprendre dans l'interaction. Analyse des médiations sémiotiques.* Aix-en-Provence et Nancy, France: Presses de l'Université de Provence & Presses Universitaires de Nancy.

Glachan, M., & Light, P. (1982). Peer interaction and learning: Can two wrongs make a right? In G. Butterworth & P. Light (Eds.), *Social cognition: Studies in the development of understanding* (pp. 238–262). Chicago: University of Chicago Press.

Grice, H. P. (1989). *Studies in the way of words*. Cambridge, MA: Harvard University Press.

Grossen, M. (1988). *L'intersubjectivité en situation de test*. Cousset, France: Delval.

Grossen, M. (1994). Theoretical and methodological consequences of a change in the unit of analysis for the study of peer interactions in a problem solving situation. *European Journal of Education, IX*(1), 159–173.

Grossen, M., Liengme Bessire, M.-J., & Perret-Clermont, A.-N. (1997). Construction de l'interaction et dynamiques socio-cognitives. In M. Grossen & B. Py (Eds.), *Pratiques sociales et médiations symboliques* (pp. 221–247). Berne, Switzerland: Peter Lang.

Guizard, N. (2001). *Etude du discours d'enfants âgés de 4 à 6 ans en situation d'explication de règles de jeu, à partir de l'analyse interlocutoire*. D. E. A. de Psychologie. Nancy, France: Université de Nancy 2.

Hartup, W. W. (1985). Relationships and their significance in cognitive development. In R. A. Hinde, A. N. Perret-Clermont, & J. Stevenson-Hinde (Eds.), *Social relationships and cognitive development* (pp. 66–81). Oxford, UK: Clarendon Press.

Keenan, E. O. (1983). Conversational competence in children. In E. Ochs & B. B. Schieffelin (Eds.), *Acquiring conversational competence* (pp. 3–25). London: Routledge, Chapman & Hall.

Kohlberg, L., Yeager, J., & Hjertholm, E. (1968). Private speech: Four studies and a review of theories. *Child Development, 39*, 691–736.

Krappmann, L. (1985). The structure of peer relationships and possible effects on school achievement. In R. A. Hinde, A. N. Perret-Clermont, & J. Stevenson-Hinde (Eds.), *Social relationships and cognitive development* (pp. 149–166). Oxford, UK: Clarendon Press.

Kruger, A. C., & Tomasello, M. (1986). Transactive discussions with peers and adults. *Developmental Psychology, 22*, 681–685.

Leadbeater, B. J. (1988). Relational processes in adolescent and adult dialogues: Assessing the intersubjective context of conversation. *Human Development, 31*, 313–326.

Mercer, N. (1995). *The guided construction of knowledge. Talk among teachers and learners*. London: Multilingual Matters.

Mercer, N. (2000). *Words & minds. How to use language to think together*. London: Routledge.

Mugny, G. (Ed.). (1991). *Psychologie sociale du développement cognitif*. Berne, Switzerland: P. Lang. (First edition 1985).

Musiol, M. (1996). La pragmatique en devenirs. *Interaction et Cognitions, 1*(1), 41–58.

Musiol, M. (2002). *Les conditions de l'analyse des troubles de la pensée dans l'interaction verbale*. Contribution au programme pragmatique et cognitif en psychopathologie. Habilitation à diriger des recherches. Paris: Université Paris VIII.

Pêcheux, M. G. (1995). Interactions parents-bébés et développement de l'intelligence: Stimulation et ajustement. In M. Robin, I. Casati, & D. Candilis-Huisman (Eds.), *La construction des liens familiaux pendant la première enfance* (pp. 129–146). Paris: Presses Universitaires de France.

Perlmutter, M., Behrend, S. D., Kuo, F., & Muller, A. (1989). Social influences of children's problem solving. *Developmental Psychology, 25*, 744–754.

Perret-Clermont, A. N. (1996). *La construction de l'intelligence dans l'interaction sociale*. Berne, Switzerland: P. Lang. (First edition 1979).

Perret-Clermont, A. N., Schubauer-Leoni, M. L., & Trognon, A. (1992). L'extorsion des réponses en situation asymétrique. *Verbum, 1–2*, 3–32.

Piaget, J. (1932). *Le jugement moral chez l'enfant*. Neuchâtel, Switzerland: Delachaux & Niestlé.

Sorsana, C. (1996). Relations affinitaires et corésolution de problème: analyse des interactions entre enfants de six-huit ans. *Interaction et Cognitions, 1*(2–3), 263–291.

Sorsana, C. (1997). Affinités enfantines et corésolution de la Tour de Hanoï. *Revue Internationale de Psychologie Sociale, 10*(1), 51–74.

Sorsana, C. (1999a). *Psychologie des interactions sociocognitives*. Paris: A. Colin (collection Synthèse).

Sorsana, C. (1999b). Stratégies socio-cognitives dans la résolution de la tour de Hanoï. In M. Gilly, J. P. Roux, & A. Trognon (Eds.), *Apprendre dans l'interaction. Analyse des médiations sémiotiques* (pp. 143–161). Aix-en-Provence & Nancy, France: Presses Universitaires de Provence & Presses Universitaires de Nancy.

Sorsana, C. (2001). Dynamiques sociales et cognitives des acquisitions. In C. Golder & D. Gaonach (Eds.), *Enseigner à des adolescents. Manuel de Psychologie* (pp. 208–233). Paris: Hachette (Education).

Sorsana, C. (2003). Comment l'interaction co-opérative rend-elle plus "savant"? Quelques réflexions concernant les conditions nécessaires au fonctionnement dialogique du conflit sociocognitif. *L'orientation scolaire et professionnelle, 32*(3), 437–473.

Sorsana, C. (2005). Croyances et habiletés conversationnelles entre enfants: réflexions à propos de la gestion dialogique des désaccords au sein des raisonnements. *Psychologie de l'Interaction, 17–18*, 39–97.

Sorsana, C., & Musiol, M. (2005). Power and knowledge. How can rationality emerge from children's interactions in a problem-solving situation? In E. Grillo (Ed.), *Power without domination. Dialogism and the empowering property of communication* (pp. 161–221). Amsterdam: John Benjamins.

Swing, S. R., & Peterson, P. L. (1982). The relation of student ability and small-group interaction to student achievement. *American Education Research Journal, 19*, 259–274.

Teasley, S. D. (1995). The role of talk in children's peer collaborations. *Developmental Psychology, 31*(2), 207–220.

Tetlock, P. E. (1983). Accountability and complexity of thought. *Journal of Personality and Social Psychology, 45*, 74–83.

Thorndyke, P., & Stasz, C. (1980). Individual differences in procedures for knowledge acquisition from maps. *Cognitive Psychology, 12*, 137–175.

Trognon, A., & Sorsana, C. (2005). Les compétences interactionnelles: formes d'exercice, bases, effets et développement. *Rééducation orthophonique, 221*, 29–56.

Vergnaud, G. (1991). Morphismes fondamentaux dans les processus de conceptualisation. In G. Vergnaud (Ed.), *Les sciences cognitives en débat* (pp. 15–28). Paris: CNRS Editions.

Webb, N. M. (1982). Group composition, group interaction, and achievement in co-operative small groups. *Journal of Educational Psychology, 74*, 475–484.

Wegerif, R., Mercer, N., & Rojas-Drummond, S. (1999). Language for the social construction of knowledge: Comparing classroom talk in Mexican preschools. *Language and Education, 13*(2), 133–150.

Wertsch, J. V. (Ed.). (1985). *Culture, communication and cognition: Vygotskian perspectives*. New York: Cambridge University Press.

Winnykamen, F. (1990). *Apprendre en imitant?* Paris: Presses Universitaires de France.

Youniss, J. (1980). *Parents and peers in social development: A Sullivan–Piaget perspective*. Chicago: University of Chicago Press.

Zajonc, R. B. (1960). The process of cognitive tuning in communication. *Journal of Abnormal and Social Psychology, 61*, 159–167.

Zimmerman, B. J., & Blom, D. E. (1983). Toward an empirical test of the role of cognitive conflict in learning. *Developmental Review, 3*, 18–38.

EUROPEAN JOURNAL OF DEVELOPMENTAL PSYCHOLOGY
2008, 5 (5), 561–584

Socio-cognitive dynamics in dyadic interaction: How do you work together to solve Kohs cubes?

Valérie Tartas
University of Toulouse, Toulouse, France, and University of Neuchâtel, Neuchâtel, Switzerland

Anne-Nelly Perret-Clermont
University of Neuchâtel, Neuchâtel, Switzerland

This study presents a detailed analysis of collaborative interaction modes employed by 9- to 10-year-old children in a spatial problem solving a task called the Kohs cubes. All the children were videotaped during non-interactive pre-test and post-test sessions (stages 1 and 4) and two types of interactive sessions: (1) novice children training with adults (stage 2); and (2) competent instruction by children, or competent children, interacting with novice children (stage 3). Dyadic sessions between competent and novice children are analysed in more detail to show how children share their involvement with the task and how they manage to solve the problem depending on their level of task competence. Three particular dimensions of these interactive sessions have been studied: (1) making strategies explicit; (2) children's task management; and (3) modes of interaction and their evolution in the course of the task resolution. Through a qualitative case-based analysis of four dyads extracted from the experiment, the results highlight the plurality and complexity of the socio-cognitive dynamics in dyadic interactions. The discussion focuses on the processes of collaborative learning involved in such interactions.

Keywords: Dyadic interactions; Learning; Kohs cubes; Socio-cognitive dynamics; Children.

Research in developmental psychology and education often aims to better understand the effects of social contexts on learning and development in children. Vygotsky (1930/1981) proposed that children's cultural development was first initiated through social interactions and later on consolidated at the psychological level: "every function in the child's cultural develop-

---

Correspondence should be addressed to Valérie Tartas, Université de Toulouse 2, Laboratoire Octogone ECCD, Pavillon de la recherche, 5 allée Antonio Machado F-31058 Toulouse Cedex France. E-mail: tartas@univ-tlse2.fr

http://www.psypress.com/edp   DOI: 10.1080/17405620701859522

ment appears twice or on two planes. First, it appears on the social plane, and then, on the psychological plane. First, it appears between people as an interpsychological category and then, within the child as an intra-psychological category.... Social relations or relations among people, genetically, underlie all the higher functions and their relationships" (Vygotsky, 1930/1981, p. 163). Although Vygotsky did not study empirically how different modes of social interaction influence our behaviours and thoughts, his writings and hypotheses opened the way for many to explore the same direction.

From such a perspective, some researchers studied adult – child interactions during learning activities, while others focused on child collaboration. Others tried to highlight which contexts may lead children to learn. Peer collaboration has been defined as "a coordinated synchronous activity that is the result of a continued attempt to construct and maintain a shared conception of a problem" (Roschelle & Teasley, 1995, p. 70). In this sense, peer collaboration (as distinct from peer tutoring) involves children working together to complete a single unified task that represents the shared meaning and communication of the group as a unit (Fawcett & Garton, 2005). Peer collaboration is not always associated with individual cognitive change (Doise & Mugny, 1984, Perret-Clermont, 1980; Tudge & Winterhoff, 1993). It is suggested that cognitive benefits may depend on a complex set of factors such as age (Hogan & Tudge, 1999), level of the partner (Gabrielle & Montecinos, 2001), confidence (Tudge, Winterhoff, & Hogan, 1996), gender (Perret-Clermont & Schubauer-Leoni, 1981; Psaltis, 2005) and the type of tasks (Phelps & Damon, 1989).

Research on child learning, however, has shown that social interactions may facilitate cognitive progress but the results are, in part, conflicting. Indeed, Perret-Clermont (1980) demonstrated that a particular type of interpersonal relationship between children, who have to solve the Piagetian liquid conservation task, is favourable to positive cognitive shifts for the partners. Such findings point to the conditions under which "two heads are better than one"(Azmitia, 1988). In contrast, Tudge (1999) showed that the social interaction between peers solving a Piagetian task may lead to cognitive regression. Other results suggest that the short-term effects of social interaction differ from their long-term effects (Howe, McWilliam, & Cross, 2005). As a result, researchers examined the efficacy of different configurations of the learning task, the role of the partners' social and cognitive characteristics and contrasted cognitive development before and after the interaction. Such an experimental setting allowed researchers to evaluate the effect of the learning context by comparing children's responses before and after the social interaction. Other interpretations, however, have been proposed. In particular, it was suggested that children may redefine the objectives of the task during the interaction and, thus, learn something that is different from what the researchers are expecting. Yet, few studies have examined how the definition of the task is discussed or redefined by the participants while they interact. Therefore, the social context of learning may or may not lead to cognitive development while also, however, contributing to the emergence of new objectives (Saxe, 1991).

It has been shown that a key element of effective peer collaboration is the active exchange of ideas through verbal communication (King, 1999; Light & Littleton, 1994; Teasley, 1995; Webb & Favier, 1999). In this sense, the total number of utterances used in interactions between two children demonstrated that it was associated with improvement in reasoning strategies or problem solving ability. Kruger (1992) showed that children who actively engaged in debate were more likely to benefit cognitively than those who were described as passive listeners. Peers who negotiated most explicitly and made more extensive use of verbal preplanning while working collaboratively tended to be the most successful at individual post-tests. It appears that the interaction needed in order to support learning and cognitive growth may allow for elaborate explanations and the asking of appropriate questions. In addition, it provides sufficient time for the partner to think and use supportive communicative skills such as listening, providing feedback and encouragement (Webb & Favier, 1999).

When studying the social facilitation of learning, it is necessary to go beyond an analysis of individual performance, before and after the social interaction, and to develop a *pluralistic perspective* of interaction that incorporates several levels of analysis (Forman & Larreamendy-Joerns, 1995). It is from such a perspective that the present research offers a study of social interaction. This *pluralistic perspective* is used in research on situated learning (Forman, Minick, & Stone, 1993; Perret-Clermont, Perret & Bell, 1991). In this tradition of research, the emphasis is put on the fact that the social context is not a static entity but is continuously created and recreated by those involved, hence developing in the course of interaction. Thus, the participants may learn the same things but not necessarily from a shared task. Different social conditions (e.g., working with a child trained by an adult or working with a peer who has not received such training) may or may not lead to cognitive progress (Grossen, Liengme Bessire, & Perret-Clermont, 1997; Nicolet, 1995; Tartas, Perret-Clermont, Marro, & Grossen, 2004).

Because a given experimental condition may lead to very different socio-cognitive dynamics, it is necessary to open the "black box" that is the social interaction in the pre- and post-test paradigm of research (Carugati, 2001). First, this will allow a closer look at what is going on when two children are solving a problem together. Second, this will enable the development of tools or methods of analysis for describing what is going on. There are different ways in which this could be done: for example, one could analyse in detail the verbal exchanges using conversational analysis to show how conversation leads to cognition (Trognon, Batt, Schwarz, Perret-Clermont,

& Marro, 2003). Another possibility would be to follow the dynamics of the interaction step by step, paying particular attention to the types of collaborative relations developed and their evolution in the course of the interaction. This latter approach was the one favoured in this study.

This work had two objectives. First, it aimed to present the exploratory results of a study on the collaborative modes of interaction children use to solve a problem. Second, it aimed to present a research process that consisted of continuously going back and forth between general laws and particular case-based analysis in order to generate new hypotheses arising from the exploration of individual variations. It is this latter process that generated the results presented here. The initial results of this study allowed the verification of the general hypothesis stating that children who have been taught by an adult during a "scaffolding" training progress learnt more than the children who did not receive such training (see Tartas et al., 2004, for more details). Based on this hypothesis of a general law tested in an experimental setting, a case study approach was developed as part of the current research in order to study the individual variations. The interaction is not static; it has a dynamic source of cognitive movements. It never develops itself in the same way. Thus, even within the same experimental condition of interaction, the instruction "working together" may not involve its participants in the same way. This is because the experimental situation does not completely define the interactive dynamics. Within each dyad, each partner will try to exploit the space given by the framework proposed in his/her own way. This will entail "chain reactions" from the partners. So, we expected that the same instruction of collective work would lead to very different socio-cognitive dynamics from one dyad to another. Nevertheless, we also expected that there would be similarities between interactions, depending on the partner's level of competency and on the type of competencies observed in the pre-test.

METHOD

Participants

One hundred 9-year-old children were tested in their school by the first author. The experimental group was composed of 27 dyads and 46 children belonged to the control group (no interaction phase). There were three groups of participants from the experimental group:

1. The Competent children (C) who demonstrated competencies to solve the task during the pre-test or stage 1.
2. The Novice children (N) who could not solve the task at the pre-test.

3. The Competent by Instruction children (CI) who were novices at the pre-test but who were then trained by an adult in stage 2 of the experiment in order to turn them into competent task solvers.

Thus, there were two types of competent children in stage 3: the children who had already constructed their competencies (C) to solve the task and the children whose modalities of acquisition of such competencies were controlled (CI) (see Figure 1). These two groups interacted in stage 3 (interaction) of the experiment. The CI children were taught so that their performances matched those of the C children. After the pre-test, and after the training for the CI children, the children worked in one of two types of dyads composed of:

1. A competent peer and a novice peer (C + N, condition 1).
2. A competent-by-instruction child and a novice peer (CI + N) (condition 2).

No tutoring was involved in these interactions since the children did not know their status or that of their partners. All the children were then tested again during a post-test session.

Materials and procedure

Stage 1 (pre-tests) and Stage 4 (post-tests).   the same material was used in these two sessions. It consisted of presenting the Kohs cubes task as it has been developed by Kohs (1923/1972). The child had to solve seventeen items of increasing levels of difficulty as the number of cubes needed to solve the task increased (from four to nine and then to sixteen cubes) and the model to reproduce became more and more complex. The scale of the model was smaller than the scale of the figure the child constructed with the cubes (0.25

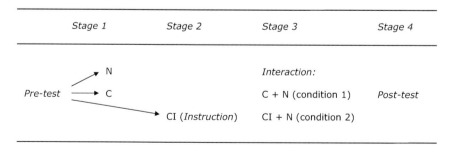

Stage 1	Stage 2	Stage 3	Stage 4
		Interaction:	
Pre-test → C ↗ N		C + N (condition 1)	Post-test
	CI (*Instruction*)	CI + N (condition 2)	

Figure 1. Experimental plan.

to 1). The researcher testing the children recorded both the time taken by the child to finish each construction and the accuracy of the construction. The test was stopped when the child made two consecutive errors.

Stage 2 (training). The training given to the CI children consisted of teaching them strategies to solve the problem using an easier model. This facilitated the task because it was at the same scale as the cubes used to construct the figure and was based on an explicit grid. Some specific strategies were given by the adult when the child encountered difficulties in solving the task on her/his own.

Stage 3 (interactions). The material used during the third stage of interaction consisted of three items each composed of sixteen cubes that the children had to construct together. These three items were new as the children had not seen them during the preceding stages. The scale used in this stage was 0.25 without any squares.

All the stages of the experiment were videotaped and the progression through the four stages took place over a week for each classroom, given that no children passed two stages on the same day.

Coding

In this study, the interactions of the four dyads were transcribed and coded in accordance with previous research the objective of which was the study of the interactive dynamics (Liengme Bessire, Grossen, Iannaccone & Perret-Clermont, 1994; Nilholm & Säljö, 1996). Three dimensions of the analysis of the interactive solving problem session (stage 3) were proposed:

1. The first dimension consisted of the active demonstration of strategies used or the fact that the strategies used were merely rendered visible to the partner. For example they could point to a cube on the model or the construction in order to draw it to their partner's attention. This pointing could also be addressed with verbal explications (for example, "Look there we are on this line, then we are going to try this block there, do you see it, so do it!"). This dimension was coded on each cube placement for each of the children.
2. The second one related to the management of the task: shared responsibility or not-shared responsibility. Was the responsibility taken by all the partners or by only one of them? It was thanks to the grid of analysis used in the third dimension that this responsibility was coded for each item during stage 3 of the interaction. Did the placement of a cube or a block come from a collective decision or an

TABLE 1

Different levels of modes of interaction of stage 3

Level	Non-competent and competent child's contributions
1	*Modelling*: one child is solving the problem whereas the other one is looking at him and sometimes being active (pointing at the model, making oral interventions, suggestions . . .) or inactive.
2	*Individual construction with no co-ordination*: each child works independently without taking notice of their partner's actions. The pattern is done without co-ordination. Eventually one child gives up his/her building in order to let his/her partner finish the pattern.
3	*Individual shared construction*: it can be summarized with this child's suggestion: "You do the bottom and I'll do the top", each child has to build a part and then have to do their construction.
4	*Alternate construction*: each child, in turn, places a block. Thus they construct the pattern together: the one who puts one block is then the one who checks her/his partner's pause. The alternating of the role can be explicit or implicit.
5	*Collaboration*: the partners construct the pattern together and consult or even confront each other, negotiating the placing of each new block. They engage clearly in negotiation to find a common solution.

individual one? How did this shared or individual functioning evolve during the interaction? The children who were developing the modes of interactions related to co-ordination (i.e., mode 3 called "individual shared construction", mode 4 called "alternate construction" and mode 5 called "collaboration") belonged to the category of shared responsibility between the partners of the task whereas the two first modes ("modelling" and "individual construction with no co-ordination") referred to an individual responsibility for the task. This notion of shared responsibility has been studied several times with respect to mother–child interactions (Wertsch, 1979; Wertsch & Hickman, 1987).

3. The third dimension concerned the modes of interaction or the patterns of the children's communications. These were analysed according to a grid composed of five levels constructed from previous work on interactive dynamics and cognitive processes (cf. Table 1). Levels 1 and 2 had the particularity of being individual modes of resolution even if the instruction was "working together" whereas the other three modes (3, 4, and 5) implied social co-ordinations.

GENERAL RESULTS

The detailed analysis of the results of the present research is still in progress. The general results that have been addressed, however, are close to those observed by Nicolet (1995). Indeed, the modality with which the subjects have acquired their expertise appears to have little influence on their cognitive development during experimentation. Nicolet (1995) did find, however, that novices who interacted with a peer made more progress than those who worked with an adult. This finding was not replicated by the present study. Moreover, in contrast to Grossen et al.'s (1997) results,[1] CI children in our study did not regress. In addition, we did not observe differences between N children who interacted with CI children and N children who interacted with C children whereas Grossen et al. (1997) reported a more important development of novices who had interacted with CI children compared to those who interacted with C children. We also observed that, overall, novices' performances on the post-test were better than the novices' performances observed by Grossen et al. (1997; see Tartas et al., 2004, for more details about this finding).

Because of the different patterns of development observed in the various experimental conditions, four dyads were chosen according to the progress observed. Such progress was evaluated by comparing the performances of children between the post-test and pre-test. It is of particular interest to focus on "extreme" dyads, which either illustrate cases where the novices significantly progressed at the post-test (around 7 items or more) or cases where novices made little or no progress. Accordingly, we chose two dyads in the first condition (C + N interactions): one where significant progress was made and one where little or no progress was observed. We also selected two dyads from the second condition (CI + N interactions) following the same selection criteria (see Table 2).

Qualitative case-based results

1. Making strategies explicit (Dimension 1)

In order to follow the interactive dynamic step by step, the focus was on the way the partners made visible and accessible their strategies to their partner. If the child rendered explicit his/her strategies to his/her partner using verbal indications or/and gestured ones, this was selected. For example, a child may direct his/her partner's attention to a specific place on the model or construction, anticipating what has to be done next. Or, for example, the child who is doing the building may construct the figure with no conveyance to his/her partner that allows him/her to understand what is being done. The question examined was: are the dyads different from each other in the way

[1]This research was conducted by Michèle Grossen with the collaboration of A. Iannaccone and M. J. Liengme Bessire thanks to the Swiss National Research Foundation: contract A.-N. Perret-Clermont, No. 11–2856190.

TABLE 2
Presentation of the four dyads

	Dyads	
	Condition 1 (C + N)	Condition 2 (CI + N)
Progress in the post-test (number of solved items compared to pre-test)	1. Martin – Thibault (+7 items)	3. Henri – Mergim (+8 items)
Stability in the post-test (number of solved items compared to pre-test)	2. Alessi – Aloys (+3 items)	4. Ismet – Fabrice (+3 items)

they rely on the active verbal and gestured demonstration of strategies? It was expected that such reliance would be present in the dyads in which competence had been acquired through scaffolding training with an adult rather than in the condition 1 dyads.

We calculated the mean number of placements with active strategy demonstrations for each of the three items of the interaction (stage 3). That is, the number of times the child verbalized or gesticulated the correct solution divided by the total number of task-solving attempts.

The competent – novice dyads (condition 1: C – N; Figure 2)

There are many differences in the way the strategies are used and demonstrated explicitly to solve the problem together. In *dyad 1* (in which the novice progresses substantially in the post-test), the articulated strategies come essentially from the competent peer who both explains and demonstrates how to solve the task. For example, Martin (C) says, "Look like that there [he points to the first line on the top of the figure], I have already done the top". These few interventions become explicit either because of the novice's request (for example, Thibault (N) asks his competent partner Martin, "Wait, wait how have you done that?!") or because the competent participant notices an error produced by his partner and wants to rectify it. For example, Martin (C) says to Thibault (N), "No no because look! [pointing to the building still in progress], there are already four blocks, look it's four by four", after this explanation, he lets Thibault correct the cube on his own and then they revert to an alternate construction style.

In *dyad 2* ("explicit communication without anticipation"), the explicit communications are used to give a general framework to initiate the interaction and the construction, "I have finished the first stair and then let's begin with another one" says Alessi (C), so Aloys (N) answers, "I do the bottom". They are concerned with what has already been done but never anticipate what remains to be done and how to do it.

The competent by instruction – novice dyads (condition 2: CI – N; Figure 3)

Dyad 3 (learning and transmitting through active demonstration, anticipation and verbalization) is clearly different from the others: the percentage of strategies explicitly used for the partner is very important for each item compared to the other dyads. Henry, who has became competent through scaffolding instruction (CI), uses the learning script proposed by the adult during stage 2 of training and proposes it to his partner. Each placement is accompanied by verification of the model and anticipation is proposed. Then he explains how he does it in order to realise his objective. He gives the first instruction at the start of the interaction, "Let's begin by the corners", then, "We had to do the line", and then he shows his partner how to divide the model with the cubes by building an entire line and verbalizing the

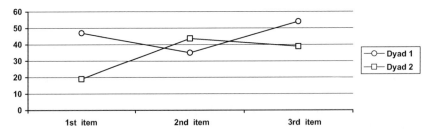

Figure 2. Percentage of active demonstrations of strategies in the course of the interaction for the dyads of the condition 1 (C − N).

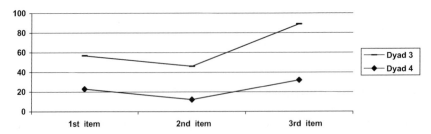

Figure 3. Percentage of active demonstrations of strategies in the course of interaction for the condition 2 dyads (CI − N).

colour and forms of the cubes. Subsequently he lets his partner practice this technique, "Now it is finished, so it's your turn, do the line", and helps him when the novice makes a mistake or doesn't know how to do it. The instances of being in anticipation are numerous from the competent partner, "We had the two lines left", so it leads the novice to anticipate too, Mergim (N), "Like that, three blocks are missing and then it will be finished!" This explains why there is an important co-constructive collaboration development in the last item (item 3). Both of the partners remain expressly in anticipation and provide explanations about how to do it. Some traces of learning within interaction can be found here.

Dyad 4 is characterized by substantial involvement of the competent peer trained through scaffolding. In dyad 4 (periodic verbal demonstrations as inner speech), the novice comes forward when he is disappointed at not having the possibility of intervening. The verbal explanations given by the competent peer seem to be addressed to himself rather than to his partner. Indeed, it seems that the competent child says what he does loudly and this seems to control his own actions on the task. His partner does not take into account the information he gives during such verbalization.

The case-based analysis shows that strategy demonstrations are irregular depending on the dyad. Additionally they not only depend on the condition under which competence is acquired but also on the way that the children interpret the instruction "working together" and give meaning to the task and their partner's actions. Nevertheless, it seems that such a tendency is characteristic of dyads where the novice's score in the post-test increases substantially compared to ones where there is no cognitive growth observed. Indeed, in dyads 1 and 3 the use of verbal explanations during the figure's construction and their reuse by the partner is more frequent than in dyads 2 and 4. That is to say that the use of demonstrations on their own is not sufficient to explain the progress for both partners. It is necessary that it becomes reused by the partner so that the active demonstration needs to be at the origin of the other partner's action. Further analysis of this particular point is needed on a large number of dyads.

2. How do the children share task control? (Dimension 2)

The notion of shared responsibility or shared task control is rooted in initial research on mother–child interaction and the analysis of knowledge transmission depending on the adult's control of the exchange (Nilholm & Säljö, 1996; Wertsch & Hickman, 1987; Wood, Bruner, & Ross, 1976). This allows an illustration of the interactive dynamics in terms of division or distribution of cognitive and manual work between the partners in order to solve the task. What takes place in terms of such a distribution between two children when they have to work together?

Condition 1: C − N dyads

Dyad 1: Frequently shared responsibility under the competent partner's impetus (Figure 4)

For Martin and Thibault "working together" means they have to tell their partner what they are doing and how to do it when the other doesn't know. Martin explains and shows how he solves the task and gives his partner a task to solve. For example, "You had to do this part of the figure on the bottom". Thibault, the novice, initiates and ends the exchange for the first item. For the second and third items, Martin initiates and ends the exchanges. For these latter two items, the control of the task is shared and there are only a few periodic moments where the building shifts to individual

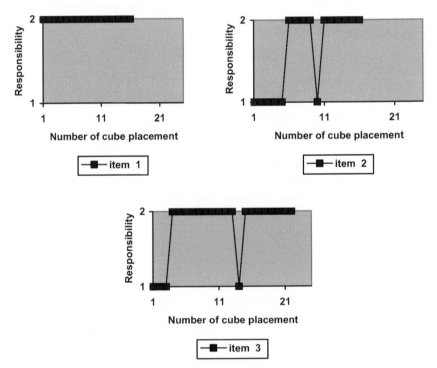

Figure 4. Shared or not-shared responsibility of the three item resolution of stage 3 interaction by dyad 1. *Notes*: 1 = not-shared responsibility; 2 = shared responsibility.

work for one or other partner. The competent child is the one who sets the objectives, reminds his partner of them in the course of the interaction and very often controls the building. The novice sometimes sets rules that he fails to maintain during the problem-solving activity that his partner then reminds him of.

Dyad 2: Periodic shared responsibility (Figure 5)

Alessi, the competent peer, initiates the work for the two first items and Aloys, N, initiates for the last one. Aloys ends the construction for the three items frequently because his partner lets him place the last cube, so it is not an actual shared responsibility. The first and last items are partly co-managed periodically by both partners. That is, the competent peer places the cubes and builds the figure whereas the novice intervenes to debate or support some placements. Item 2 is managed completely by the competent peer with the novice faulting him for doing it alone.

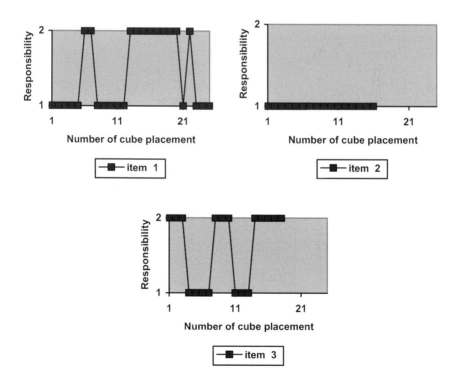

Figure 5. Shared or not-shared responsibility of the three item resolution of stage 3 interaction by dyad 2. *Notes*: 1 = not-shared responsibility; 2 = shared responsibility.

The competent – novice (C – N) dyads are very different in their means of distributing task responsibility. The patterns according to this criterion "shared responsibility or not-shared responsibility" are very different depending on the items (e.g., the distribution is not the same on the first, second or third one) and the way each partner engages in the work and the role he assigns to his partner.

Condition 2: The competent by instruction – novice (CI – N) dyads

Dyad 3: Invitation to construct—a shared-task responsibility (Figure 6)

Shared responsibility characterizes this dyad. The competent peer, who has acquired competence via instruction, makes his work explicit to his partner and asks him to build the figure with him. It seems that learning

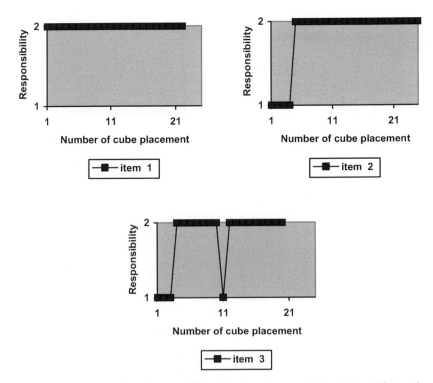

Figure 6. Shared or not-shared responsibility of the three item resolution of stage 3 interaction by dyad 3. *Notes:* 1 = not-shared responsibility; 2 = shared responsibility.

with the adult allows him to understand which question has to be asked in order to solve the task and what to do to answer it. Then he draws his partner into this learning logic, which makes the latter begin to become an active dyad member. The competent partner initiates the three items and ends the first one, whereas the final two ones are finished by both partners.

Dyad 4: When the responsibility becomes shared increasingly throughout the interaction (Figure 7)

The two modes of task control are found in this dyad. For the first two items, it alternates between an individualistic (i.e., not-shared) control managed by the competent child and a shared control between the partners. The competent child first takes charge of the building and initiates the construction of the three items. Then the novice reminds him of the instruction "working together", which subsequently has an effect on the

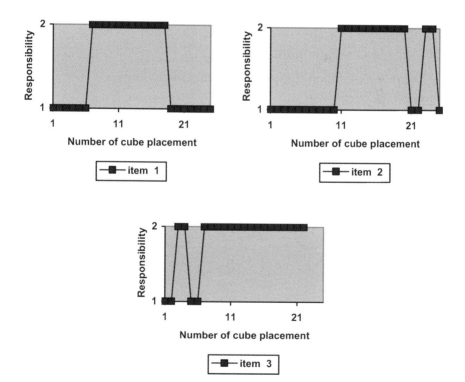

Figure 7. Shared or not-shared responsibility of the three item resolution of stage 3 interaction by dyad 4. *Notes:* 1 = not-shared responsibility; 2 = shared responsibility.

mode of task management. It leads to a collaborative mode of management between the children: each of them alternately placing a cube or two. The final stage of item 1 is then managed by the competent peer alone, who checks his placements compared to the model and makes corrections if necessary. This solitary mode of management continues onto the start of item 2 and then the novice intervenes in order to offer some solutions. The control of item 3 is socially distributed. It is more often *both* of the partners who end the task for the three items. The development towards an increasing shared-task control appears in the third item's course of resolution.

3. Different modes of interactions

The analysis that follows examines the ways the four dyads construct the interaction in order to solve the task. This is in accordance with the five levels of analysis elaborated from different works on social interaction made in Neuchâtel and the works in socio-cultural psychology on adult–child relations (Wertsch & Hickman, 1987).

The dyads C – N (condition 1)

Dyad 1: Resolution through different collaborative dynamics (Figure 8)

The interaction evolves a great deal in the course of the resolution of the three items. Mode 3 (individual alternated construction), modes 4 and 5 (where the activity of resolution is more co-elaborated) are the more

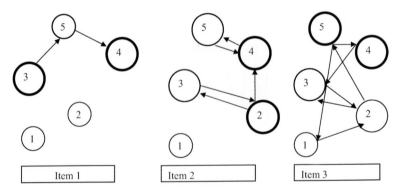

Figure 8. Evolution of the modes of interaction in dyad 1 (Thibault–Martin). *Notes:* 1: Modelling; 2: Individual construction with no co-ordination; 3: Individual shared construction; 4: Alternate construction; 5: Collaboration.

frequently used. The approaches to co-elaboration (mode 5) are never the same during the resolution of the three items. There are, indeed, important interactive dynamic styles used by this dyad in order to solve the problem. The two first items are solved in two minutes and the third one in three minutes.

Dyad 2: When collaboration is too periodic (Figure 9)

In dyad 2, interaction mode 2 remains consistent in the resolution of the three items. Indeed, the competent child seems to take responsibility for the building (mode 2) with moments of alternated construction between the partners (mode 4) or co-elaborations (mode 5). The move from mode 2 to mode 4 or 5 is more often due to the detection of an error. The children work fast on these items, which are resolved in two minutes. There is little evolution in the way they solve the problem.

The dyads CI − N (condition 2)

Dyad 3: Learning through collaborative dynamics (Figure 10)

Modes 4 and 5 are particularly characteristic of the interactive dynamics of this dyad. There is more diversity of interaction modes during the resolution of the third item. The placements of cubes are social constructions distributed between the partners. They are more often accompanied by verbal explanations (from the competent peer), which are subsequently reused by the novice. The first two items are solved in five minutes and in six

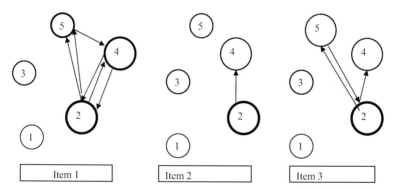

Figure 9. Evolution of the modes of interaction in dyad 2 (Alessi–Aloys). *Notes*: 1: Modelling; 2: Individual construction with no co-ordination; 3: Individual shared construction; 4: Alternate construction; 5: Collaboration.

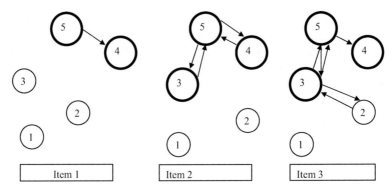

Figure 10. Evolution of the modes of interaction in dyad 3 (Henri–Mergim). *Notes*: 1: Modelling; 2: Individual construction with no co-ordination; 3: Individual shared construction; 4: Alternate construction; 5: Collaboration.

for the last one. In the course of the exchange a "proximal zone of development," as Vygotsky (1978) proposed, is elaborated in the sense that the competent partner manages to create a space for learning. This initially allows his partner to learn the task solution first under his control and then he provides more space to allow his partner to solve the problem on his own. The novice relies on it and even, at times, is the one who reminds his partner of his initially proposed rules and strategies. The interactive dynamic develops in the course of the collaborative work.

Dyad 4: When collaboration is not long enough (Figure 11)

The two first items are solved with the same modes of task management by the partners. The building is first independent without co-ordination (mode 2) and then becomes alternate construction (mode 4). That is to say that each child places a cube, one at a time, and controls his building as well as his partner's. Then there is an individual mode with periodic moments of collaborative resolution (i.e., the individual approach to building becomes collaborative when the children try to assemble them—mode 3). The last item relies on a co-elaboration (i.e., negotiation is used to solve the problem). The novice does not make any benefit from the interaction, as his post-test shows, although the children manage to construct periodic spaces for negotiation. With the last item, it seems as if the novice can begin to learn strategies but also that it is too short to be able to fully grasp and reuse them subsequently when he is alone facing the task. The time used to solve the three items varies little (4 minutes for item 1; 5 minutes for item 2; and 3 minutes 40 seconds for item 3).

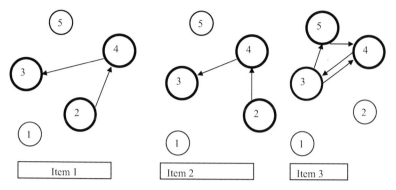

Figure 11. Evolution of the modes of interaction in dyad 4 (Ismet – Fabrice). *Notes*: 1: Modelling; 2: Individual construction with no co-ordination; 3: Individual shared construction; 4: Alternate construction; 5: Collaboration.

DISCUSSION

The results, highlighted from this detailed case-based description of four focal dyads, show all the complex and diverse ways of interpreting, and performing, the instruction "working together" given at the beginning of stage 3. In this sense, they confirm the hypothesis. In order to explore this diversity, the case-based analyses show the diverse instruction interpretations by the different participants.

When examining the dimension called "active demonstrations", we notice that some of the dyads try to verbalize their actions as they place a cube. They are preparing the subsequent actions in order to explain to their partner what to do with the cubes to reproduce the model. In this sense, the qualitative sequential analysis proposed in this paper fits in with the quantitative results on effective verbal interactions between peers (King, Staffiero, & Adelgais, 1998). The present sequential analysis, however, enables the ability to go further and shows that strategy verbalization seems to have multiple functions in the different dyads. For example, in dyad 3, effective verbal interactions (i.e., providing explanations to solve the problem, asking appropriate questions, using supportive communicative skills) allow the novice to understand the actions and ways of solving the task given by his competent partner (instructed). They have a communicative function as well as an attentional one. They may regulate the behaviour of the competent partner (function of regulation of the action as Luria, 1961, proposed). This latter function is used in some of the dyads: the strategy verbalization reflects inner speech, which allows the children to control their own behaviour. This kind of language was found particularly in dyads (condition 2) comprised of a child competent by instruction (CI) and a novice. It is as if the interaction of stage 3 allows the competent partner to solidify the strategies learned from the adult more often, without any intention of communicating them to their partner. Otherwise, if they make sense, they could sometimes be reused by the novice. But generally these verbal strategies seem to help the one verbalizing them more than the one hearing them.

Making the strategies explicit for the other seems to be a necessary condition in solving the Kohs cubes together, but not in learning them and ensuring their use by the partner. The children, except those in dyad 3, do not automatically verbalize their strategies but do so when the novice intervenes and asks his/her partner how he/she has done something or what he/she has to do. The verbalization can also occur in reaction to an error discovered by the competent peer (C or CI). These verbalizations have hybrid functions that should be studied further. This is to examine whether adult-trained children (CI), who are invited to verbalize their strategies, use it to regulate their actions more frequently than the competent children (C). Additionally it would be of interest to know the respective influences on the partner. It would allow the contribution of some precision on the part of the children who learn strategies from the interaction and enable a distinction between how the children learn and how they communicate. These results are supportive of the research of Fawcett and Garton (2005) in which they have shown that children who were instructed to talk in a particular way in a collaborative phase were subsequently able to complete a relatively greater number of items from pre- to post-test compared to those children in dyads where there were minimal verbal interactions.

The analysis of distributed or shared task responsibility (i.e., dimension 2) between the partners highlights the important diversity of the management of the task control. Some competent children (C or CI) found it easier to solve the task on their own rather than solve it with the novice child. This is because taking the other into account was time consuming and cognitively demanding. This analysis shows that the meaning of the task develops in the course of the resolution of the three items. The moves in the task control may, more often, come from an explicit demand by the novice who reminds his partner of the instruction given (i.e., "working together"). This directs the competent partner to set aside individual work and proceed to collaborative. This responsibility of the task control could be analysed by looking at who initiates and ends the activity for the three items. Do the children take the initiative for beginning the task and ending it or does only one of them assume this responsibility? It seems that the analysis using such a criterion shows some regularity when it is done on a large number of dyads (see Psaltis, 2005).

The sequential analyses of the development of interaction modes (dimension 3) during the three item solutions are of particular interest for collaborative learning research. The results show that some of the children directly engage in the interaction to find a shared problem solution. In these cases, the ways to reach this shared solution are then diversified and varied. For example, one way is to count the number of cubes and then equally share them. Then there is alternate placement of a cube or a block (mode 4) or in some cases, the children construct a part of the figure independently and then try to assemble it with their partner (mode 3). Subsequently, negotiation is initiated when the building does not fit the model, so the children may sometimes move to a co-elaboration mode of resolution (mode 5). Some of them first co-elaborate (mode 5) during the first placements of blocks and try to find a common explanation of the situation and work together in order to attain the solution. Others, although receiving the same instruction (i.e., "working together to solve the problem"), engage in individual work with an inactive partner or one who loses direction and therefore adopts his partner's way of solving the task (modes 1 and 2).

The children who solve Kohs cubes move from one interaction mode to another as they construct the figure while the meaning of the task changes also, whatever the experimental conditions. The implicit objectives each child places on the task leads him/her to interpret the instruction as a task to accomplish with the partner even if it takes time, it is difficult to work with the other, and even if they make errors and are obliged to begin again. Conversely, for others, the speed of construction or finishing first is tantamount. The fact that the pre-test is chronometric may lead to such an interpretation of the instruction, so the partner chooses to work on his own rather than with his partner in order to finish quickly. The task did not have the same meaning for all the partners and they did not manage to agree on the definition of the situation. It will be interesting, in further analysis, to follow what the children interpret and understand of the task in the pre-test stage and how this comprehension develops in the subsequent experimental stages. There is, then, a necessity to develop further studies using longitudinal approaches on all the experimental stages. In this sense, the sharing of the same task objectives (e.g., to do the construction quickly or not to add a block without the approval of one's partner, etc.) and the interaction modes used to solve the task will need to be studied.

Moreover what such sequential analyses offer, in addition to opening new questions, is mainly to focus on the process where an individual cognitive solution becomes a collaborative shared one. It seems that it is rather in the move from one interaction mode to another that the learning may occur rather than being a part of a particular mode of interaction. So, what is needed now is the exploration of the changes or "crossings" from one mode to another and to attempt analysis of which moves, or patterns of moves, are likely to be the important ones in cognitive growth.

The three dimensions of the co-operative learning activity analysed here represent some elements of a larger research program rather than complete results. At this stage of our research, we hope to contribute to the development of some detailed analyses in order to allow taking into account the complexity of reality to better understand opportunities to learn.

REFERENCES

Azmitia, M. (1988). Peer interaction and problem solving. When two heads are better than one? *Child Development*, *59*, 87–96.

Carugati, F. (2001). Interactions, déstabilisations, conflits. In A. N. Perret-Clermont & M. Nicolet (Eds.), *Interagir et connaître. Enjeux et régulations sociales dans le développement cognitif* (pp. 103–112). Paris: L'Harmattan.

Doise, W., & Mugny, G. (1984). *The social development of the intellect*. Oxford, UK: Pergamon.

Fawcett, L. M., & Garton, A. F. (2005). The effect of peer collaboration on children's problem solving ability. *British Journal of Educational Psychology*, *75*, 157–169.

Forman, E. A., & Larreamendy-Joerns, J. (1995). Learning in the context of peer collaboration: A pluralistic perspective on goals and expertise. *Cognition and Instruction*, *13*(4), 549–564.

Forman, E. A., Minick, N., & Stone, C. A. (Eds.). (1993). *Contexts for learning: Sociocultural dynamics in children's development*. New York: Oxford University Press.

Gabriele, A. J., & Montecinos, C. (2001). Collaborating with a skilled peer: The influence of achievement goals and perceptions of partners' competence on the participation of learning of low achieving activities. *Journal of Experimental Education*, *69*(2), 152–167.

Grossen, M., Liengme Bessire, M.-J., & Perret-Clermont, A.-N. (1997). Construction de l'interaction et dynamiques sociocognitives. In M. Grossen & B. Py (Eds.), *Pratiques sociales et médiations symboliques* (pp. 221–247). Berne, Switzerland: Peter Lang.

Hogan, D., & Tudge, J. (1999). Implications of Vygotsky's theory for peer learning. In A. O'Donnell & A. King (Eds.), *Cognitive perspectives on peer learning* (pp. 39–65). Hillsdale, NJ: Lawrence Erlbaum Associates, Inc.

Howe, C., McWilliam, D., & Cross, G. (2005). Chance favours only the prepared mind: Incubation and the delayed effects of peer collaboration. *British Journal of Psychology*, *96*, 67–93.

King, A. (1999). Discourse patterns for mediating peer learning. In A. M. O'Donnell & A. King (Eds.), *Cognitive perspectives on peer learning* (pp. 87–117). Mahwah, NJ: Lawrence Erlbaum Associates, Inc.

King, A., Staffieri, A., & Adelgais, A. (1998). Mutual peer tutoring: Effects of structuring tutorial interaction to scaffold peer learning. *Journal of Educational Psychology*, *90*(1), 134–152.

Kohs, S. C. (1923). *Intelligence measurement*. New York: Macmillan.

Kruger, A. C. (1992). The effect of peer and adult–child transactive discussions on moral reasoning. *Merrill-Palmer Quarterly*, *38*, 191–211.

Liengme Bessire, M.-J., Grossen, M., Iannaccone, A., & Perret-Clermont, A.-N. (1994). Social comparison of expertise: Interactional patterns and dynamics of instruction. In H. C. Foot, C. J. Howe, A. K. Tolmie, & D. A. E. Warden (Eds.), *Group and interactive learning* (pp. 471–476). Southampton Boston: Computational Mechanics Publishers.

Light, P., & Littleton, K. (1994). Cognitive approaches to group work. In P. Kutnick & C. Rogers (Eds.), *Group in schools* (pp. 87–103). London: Cassell.

Luria, A. R. (1961). *The role of speech in the regulation of normal and abnormal behavior*. New York: Irvington.

Nicolet, M. (1995). *Dynamiques relationnelles et processus cognitifs*. Neuchâtel, Switzerland: Delachaux et Niestlé.

Nilholm, C., & Säljö, R. (1996). Co-action, situation definitions and socio-cultural experience. A study of problem solving in mother–child interaction. *Learning and Instruction, 6*(4), 325–344.

Phelps, E., & Damon, W. (1989). Problem solving with equals: Peer collaborations as a context for learning mathematics and spatial concepts. *Journal of Educational Psychology, 81*(4), 639–646.

Perret-Clermont, A.-N. (1980). *Social interaction and cognitive development in children*. London: Academic Press.

Perret-Clermont, A.-N., Perret, J.-F., & Bell, N. (1991). The social construction of meaning and cognitive activity in elementary school children. In L. B. Resnick & S. D. Teasley (Eds.), *Perspectives on socially shared cognition* (pp. 41–62). Washington, DC: American Psychological Association.

Perret-Clermont, A.-N., & Schubauer-Leoni, M.-L. (1981). Conflict and co-operation as opportunities for learning. In W. P. Robinson (Ed.), *Communication in development* (pp. 203–234). New York: Academic Press.

Psaltis, C. (2005). *Social relations and cognitive development: The influence of conversation types and representations of gender*. Unpublished PhD, University of Cambridge, UK.

Roschelle, J., & Teasley, S. D. (1995). The construction of shared knowledge in collaborative problem solving. In C. O'Malley (Ed.), *Computer supported collaborative learning* (pp. 69–97). Berlin, Germany: Springer.

Saxe, G. B. (1991). *Culture and cognitive development: Studies in mathematical understanding*. Hillsdale, NJ: Lawrence Erlbaum Associates, Inc.

Tartas, V., Perret-Clermont, A.-N., Marro, P., & Grossen, M. (2004). Interactions sociales et appropriation de stratégies par l'enfant pour résoudre un problème: quelles méthodes? *Bulletin de psychologie, 57*(1), 469, Numéro Spécial Développement et fonctionnement: perspective historico-culturelle, 111–115.

Teasley, S. D. (1995). The role of talk in children's peer collaboration. *Developmental Psychology, 31*(2), 207–220.

Tudge, J. R. H. (1999). Processes and consequences of peer collaboration: A Vygotskian analysis. In P. Lloyd & C. E. Fernyhough (Eds.), *Lev Vygotsky, Critical Assessments* (Vol. 3, pp. 195–221). London: Routledge.

Tudge, J. R. H., & Winterhoff, P. A. (1993). Vygotsky, Piaget & Bandura: Perspectives on the relation between the social world and the cognitive development. *Human Development, 39*, 61–81.

Tudge, J. R. H., Winterhoff, P. A., & Hogan, D. M. (1996). The consequences of collaborative problem solving with and without feed-back. *Child Development, 67*, 2892–2909.

Trognon, A., Batt, M., Schwarz, B., Perret-Clermont, A. N., & Marro, P. (2003). L'apprentissage dans l'interaction: Essai d'analyse interlocutoire. In A. Herzig, B. Chaib-Draa, & P. Mathieu (Eds.), *Modèles formels de l'interaction* (pp. 229–240). Toulouse, France: Cépaduès.

Vygotsky, L. S. (1978). *Mind in society. The development of higher psychological processes*. Cambridge, MA: Harvard University Press.

Vygotsky, L. S. (1981). The genesis of higher mental functions. In J. Wertsch (Ed.), *The concept of activity in Soviet psychology* (pp. 147–188). Armonk, NY: Sharpe, Inc. (Originally published 1930).

Webb, N. M., & Favier, S. (1999). Developing productive group interaction in middle school mathematics. In A. O'Donnell & A. King (Eds.), *Cognitive perspectives on peer learning* (pp. 117–149). Hillsdale, NJ: Lawrence Erlbaum Associates, Inc.

Wertsch, J. (1979). From social interaction to higher psychological processes: A clarification and application of Vygotsky's theory. *Human Development, 22,* 1–22.

Wertsch, J., & Hickman, M. (1987). Problem solving in social interaction: A microgenetic analysis. In M. Hickman (Ed.), *Social and functional approaches to language and thought* (pp. 81–98). San Diego, CA: Academic Press.

Wood, D. J., Bruner, J. S., & Ross, G. (1976). The role of tutoring in problem solving. *Journal of Child Psychology and Psychiatry, 17,* 89–100.

EUROPEAN JOURNAL OF DEVELOPMENTAL PSYCHOLOGY
2008, 5 (5), 585–608

Collaborative writing devices, types of co-operation, and individual acquisitions

Isabelle Olry-Louis

University of Paris 3, and INETOP/CNAM, Paris, France

Isabelle Soidet

INETOP/CNAM, Paris, France

What makes collaboration constructive from a cognitive point of view? After having examined the problem of the analysis of co-operative interactions and having defined of what the collaborative methods of learning from texts consist, the present article seeks to answer this question. This study considered two sources of variation in the learning task, using social science texts: on the one hand, partial or complete collaborative writing conditions are varied so as to examine the most favourable for learning, and on the other hand, the types of co-operation are analysed in small groups and individuals, in order to identify the most productive types, from the point of view of future acquisitions.

Keywords: Co-operation; Interaction roles; Socio-cognitive interactions; Learning from texts; Collaborative writing.

As a research object, learning through interaction highlights a series of questions. What can be learnt through interaction? Who learns? Through which processes? What are the individual, didactic, and social conditions of their implementation? Which are the interlocutory "traces"? The answer to these questions can have many repercussions, particularly in the field of teaching. For this purpose, educational interactions were studied with reference to various dimensions, in particular the so-called social dimension, defined by the nature of the interpersonal relationships, and the so-called physical dimension, which regroups the objects and artefacts that can be available to solve problems and to communicate (Baker, Brixhe, & Quignard, 2002).

Correspondence should be addressed to Isabelle Olry-Louis, Université Paris 3 Sorbonne nouvelle, 13 rue Santeuil 75 231 Paris Cedex 05, France. E-mail: Isabelle.olry@wanadoo.fr

http://www.psypress.com/edp
DOI: 10.1080/17405620701859563

The research focuses here on examining who learns and how, considering the variability of the work groups, characterized by the way they function and that of the individuals, identified through the roles they play. The study relates to learning through texts, the task consisting in writing the synthesis of a documentary file under various conditions relative to the physical dimension of interactions, and which we will call "collaborative writing conditions". By varying the writing conditions, more or less collaborative, which are proposed to pupils from secondary schools, we analyse, on the bases of linguistic indicators, which are specific to the social dimension, and the types of co-operation used in each condition, in each work group and by each participant, in order to identify those that appear to be the most productive from the point of view of future acquisitions.

Let us first examine what learning through interaction means and how it is possible to analyse co-operative interactions, before we present the collaborative learning devices through texts.

LEARNING THROUGH CO-OPERATIVE INTERACTION

Tutoring interactions and interactions within peer groups

Usually, a distinction is made between the study of tutoring interactions and interactions within peer groups. If one considers the nature of the exchanges, this distinction is well founded.

Indeed, *tutoring interactions* are generally observed within expert–beginner asymmetrical dyads in which the role of the expert—an adult or a well-trained peer who is able to master the task—is to transmit knowledge to the beginner.

In his/her interventions, the expert must simultaneously pay attention to the speech, the learning object, and its adjustment to the beginner (Chi, Siler, & Jeong, 2004; Graesser, Persson, & Magliano, 1995). For the beginner, the behaviours studied are primarily related to the *assistance* requests. Not only can the expert–beginner's interactions be qualified as asymmetrical, but also the mechanisms that enable each person to find a cognitive benefit through the other person: the expert, by clarifying the contents for the beginner, profits from a tutor effect, while the beginner learns thanks to appropriate assistance (Bruner, 1983; Kuhn, Shaw, & Felton, 1997).

The symmetrical interactions within peer groups are characterized, a priori, by a symmetry of competences and roles, the task consisting in solving a problem with others. Unlike the preceding ones, the interactions between the participants are no longer one way but become multidirectional, and the learning mechanisms, presumably equivalent for all, are constrained by the *co-operation* behaviours (Gillies & Ashman, 1998). This can be defined as the way in which the members of a given dyad or group, confronted with a particular learning situation, gather their strengths, their know-how, and their knowledge to reach their goal (Olry-Louis, 2003). Co-operation can be prescribed through an "experimental contract", which invites the partners to co-ordinate their activities and produce a common answer (Doise & Mugny, 1997; Perret-Clermont, 1996). It can be the subject of educational interventions aiming at optimizing collaborative work on the cognitive and social levels (Cohen, 1994; Johnson, Johnson, Stanne, & Garibaldi, 1990; Webb, 1989). It can also be appreciated a posteriori by means of an analysis of the dialogues (Sorsana, 2003). These two last perspectives are all the more interesting, as several authors have underlined (Crook, 1995; Gillies, 2004; Grossen, 1994; Joiner, Littleton, Faulkner, & Miell, 2000), the co-operative behaviours are not spontaneous, the stake of future research is to enable a better understanding of the social conditions in which the co-operative relationships emerge and develop.

Upon first analysis, the interactions that mediate the tutorial and group learning thus appear to be different in nature. However, tutoring is also a fundamentally co-operative enterprise in that what is taught is the product of an interaction (Brixhe, Marro-Clément & Picard, 1996). Conversely, the work within a group is also composed of requests and answers formulated in terms of assistance (Webb & Mastergeorge, 2003; Webb, Troper, & Fall, 1995). Each interaction that aims at training is thus partly made up of tutoring, and of co-operative and individual behaviours. Thus, along with other authors (cf. Grossen, 1994; Grossen & Bachmann, 2000), we think that it is essential to bring together different fields of study related to tutoring and co-operative interaction. Indeed, if it is presupposed that certain types of interaction can generate new cognitive constructions, then it is necessary to analyse thoroughly the cognitive and discursive processes (meaning negotiating, supporting, reformulating, etc.) at stake in the tutoring interaction as well as in the peer group interactions. However, the fact of bringing them together leads to methodological problems, which we will examine.

Analysis of co-operative interactions

To the question: "How may one describe co-operative interactions *a posteriori?*", several alternative answers can be proposed to the researchers. We will distinguish three of them.

A first set of Anglo-Saxon studies calls upon *objective methods* to carry out a systematic coding of interactions starting from preset categories (Gillies, 2004; Gillies & Ashman, 1996; King, Staffieri, & Adelgais, 1998; Shachar & Sharan, 1994; Teasley, 1995; Webb et al., 1995). These methods have the advantage of enabling a direct connection of learning performances with the characteristics of the interaction in which we are interested.

The link established by Cohen (1994) between the frequency of verbal interactions and the learning process has been developed by Webb's work (Webb, 1989; Webb et al., 1995), which shows that it is mainly requested explanations, at a deep level and followed up by an effective implementation on behalf of the applicant, that are correlated to later success. In this kind of work, precise qualitative variables relating to the type of the interaction are located for each subject and are considered as being likely to mediate the relationship between the co-operative interaction and the result of the learning process. A variety of inter-individual intervention modes can be highlighted, and one seeks to appreciate the efficiency of each of them from the point of view of cognitive constructions. As they rely on verifiable criteria, these methods are precious. On the other hand, their main disadvantage is that they leave aside structural and temporal phenomena, which could inform about the emergence and the development of co-construction processes.

Another set of works is based on *interpretative methods*. By taking the dyad or group in which the participants interact as the analysis unit, and not the individuals themselves, the authors seek to understand how the children use verbal expression to think together (cf. Kumpulainen & Mutanen, 1999). They have the particularity of highlighting global characterizations of linguistic operations; Mercer's research (1996) constitutes a good example of this kind of work. Wondering about the type of words that most likely lead to the construction of knowledge, he carried out an analysis that took into account the linguistic, psychological, and cultural dimensions. He thus underlined three ways of talking to oneself and of thinking: the *"disputational talk"*, characterized by short dialogues made up of assertions and counter-assertions aiming at criticizing and at deciding; the *"cumulative talk"*, easily identified by its repetitive form, which provides the possibility of having common knowledge; and the *"exploratory talk"*, composed of clarification requests followed by explanations and justifications, which enables the partners to engage in constructive criticism of the ideas of others. These kinds of verbal exchanges have been used in other studies (for example, Arvaja, Häkkinen, Eteläpelto, & Rasku-Puttonen, 2000), as were the interactive dynamics described by Gilly, Fraisse, and Roux (1988), the contents of which is very close. According to us, the limits of these studies lies in the arbitrary choice of corpus extracts, in the non-systematic character of the analyses and, in a more general way, in the absence of reference to a theory of dialogue.

A third set of works, which has been developed in Europe, is not touched by the two previous criticisms, insofar as it is based on a *logical analysis of the interlocution* (Gilly, Roux, & Trognon, 1999). Studying step by step the structure of the dialogues in a given conversational sequence, it enables one to describe how cognitions occur in the conversation, within the framework of a problem-solving situation (Trognon & Batt, 2003). This kind of sequential analysis can also enable one to appreciate the co-operative character of the conversations a posteriori. Defining co-operation as "a *levelling relationship between 2 or* n *individuals who create a finalized social space for a task and who build a functional interdependence in order to reach this goal*", Sorsana (2003) offered to look for interlocutory indicators in the configuration of the sequence. The latter is characterized by "the exchange" within the co-operative dyads, in which one observes alternating initiatives, very few dissensions, converging view points, and by "the intervention" in the non-co-operative dyads, in which one notices frequent oppositions, formulated through directing statements, imposing ideas or actions without having the interlocutor's approval. As it results from a pragmatic theory of conversation and it seeks to be rigorous on the logical level, this method is complex to implement and, according to us, should be used exclusively for dialogue analysis.

In this part, we voluntarily decided not to distinguish the studies carried out on dyads and those carried out on small groups. But if we come to the methodological problems linked to the analysis of co-operative interactions, we meet a major obstacle due to the fact that the dialogues within the dyads cannot be studied in the same way as the "polylogues" in work groups. Indeed, a "dialogue" can be subjected to a thorough analysis in which it is possible to examine how the logic is co-constructed by considering, for example, adjacent interventions initiative/reactive pairs. The "trilogues" and the "polylogues", as plural exchanges collected in situations bringing together at least three individuals, reveal many problems—the co-locution phenomena, the hierarchization of the various partners, and the emergence of coalitions or rejection phenomena—which renew the conversational approach, while breaking the traditional framework of face-to-face communication, the concept of taking turns in a conversation, and the division of the interaction itself (Grosjean & Traverso, 2002).

Because of all these difficulties, we consider that it is preferable for the moment, without denying in any way the contribution of sequential methods, to privilege the systematic coding of the linguistic behaviours in order to try to describe the trilogues and polylogues collected during training in groups. Having discussed this point, several questions remain (Hoyles & Forman, 1995; Kumpalainen & Mutanen, 1999). Which information must be analysed in co-operative learning? With which analysis unit: individual, dyadic, group? Using qualitative or quantitative variables? How are we to describe the interaction in a dynamic way? Should one consider what each one of the partners does, and what is co-constructed by them?

Let us recall that on the theoretical level, learning through interaction is considered as a set of intrapersonal and interpersonal processes, the main theoretical question being precisely based on the reciprocal transition from interpersonal processes to intrapersonal processes (Vygotsky, 1934/1985). According to us, the methodological consequence of this is that the analysis units must focus on the individual as well as on the group in which they interact. Concerning the individual, it is advisable to look for traces of the learning process and the types of participation of each one in the group. In the peer group, the modes of collaboration must be characterized and placed in relation to the learning performances.

The objective of the present empirical study was to analyse the operating modes of individuals and small working groups, considering effective performances. Such a project cannot be outlined without reference to a theory of the learning task. Because it is little structured and highly complex, thus being able to give place to various problem-solving modes, even with confrontations, a learning through texts task was selected. It consists in making a synthesis, in the shape of a collaborative essay, a documentary file read by every one, and then an evaluation of what has been learnt from the texts. The theories related to learning through texts, which we will examine in the following section, should also enable us to think about the way in which individual resources and resources co-constructed during the transactions can be mobilized in various collaborative devices.

LEARNING THROUGH TEXTS

Learning through texts requires complex processes (McNamara, Kintsch, Butler Songer, & Kintsch, 1996; Voss & Ney Silfies, 1996), which we will present by referring to the particular case of the multiple documents proposed in social sciences.

In the field of *text comprehension*, the models suggested postulate the existence of specific cognitive processes, some of which would ensure the construction of macro-cultural representations. These processes enable the reader to build his own interpretation of the text on the basis of generalization and inferences, which gradually lead him to condense the relevant information. A situation model is progressively elaborated and combines the new information with the reader's initial knowledge, and particularizes it in order to account for the space – time context in which the events described take place. The situation model influences in turn the later data processes and enables the acquisition of new knowledge (Kintsch, 1988; Van Dijk & Kintsch, 1983). The situation model built would be particularly stable in the case of reading several texts provided on the same topic, offering to the person the opportunity of locating progressively the convergences and divergences between the sources (Carretero & Voss, 1994). For the texts relating to social sciences, the clearest acquisitions can be noticed in the case where, on the one hand, the documents present several aspects of a same event, certain points of view being contradictory, and, on the other hand, the readers activate their processes of indexation, corroboration, contextualization, and characterization of the sources that are typically used by the experts (Britt & Aglinskas, 2002; Rouet, Britt, Mason, & Perfetti, 1996; Wiley & Voss, 1999; Wineburg, 1991).

In the field of *text production*, the drafting processes related to planning or setting into text are very dependant on the script writer's preliminary knowledge, which enables them to focus entirely on the organization of the contents, by limiting the memory recovery time (Fayol, 1997). This same knowledge is likely to be transformed or re-elaborated during the drafting, under the effect of the intense cognitive activity that it involves, especially for well-trained script writers (cf. Scardamalia & Bereiter, 1991). The writings produced by beginners in social sciences show a low level of integration of the information provided, the organization of the text is not explicit, and we can notice misinterpretations (E. L. Baker, 1994). In contrast, those produced by experts are characterized by an explicit detailed plan, a well-built argumentation, and the presentation of causal relations between the elements mentioned (Voss, Greene, Post, & Penner, 1983). Such a drafting activity gives the opportunity to fix, more surely and in a more articulate way, the knowledge evoked in the text (Greene, 1994). All things considered, in drafting as well as in text comprehension, it seems that those who achieve the most difficult tasks benefit the most from the point of view of knowledge (Scardamalia & Bereiter, 1991). If we wish to articulate these two activities functionally, one must wonder which reading tasks, followed by which writing tasks, would lead to the best level of comprehension. To this question, Wiley and Voss (1999) plead for a multiple documents reading task, followed by a well-argued written essay task.

If we focus on what Hayes (1996) calls "the social environment of the task", some recent works aimed at studying comprehension and/or text production processes in a socio-cognitive perspective. They made the assumption that confronting one's representation of a text or an essay with someone else's would have positive effects induced by the transition from intrapersonal processes to interpersonal ones. More precisely, to discuss a text would facilitate the process of collecting relevant information and articulate it in a coherent way. By enabling the script writers to verbalize their goals and their drafting strategies, it would compensate for the absence of feedback inherent to any individual drafting. The question of the optimal collaborative device remains. Braaksma, Rijlardaam, van den Berg, and Van Hout-Wolters (2004) showed that a simple learning through observation affects time organization and the quality of the text produced, after having been exposed to a model. For some people, the revision processes are maximized when they are used by dyads concerning a text written by one of the partners (Zammuner, 1995). For others, the product of dyadic drafting is not necessarily better than that of an individual drafting (Roussey, Farioli, & Piolat, 1992).

The results of these studies do not enable us to reveal the most profitable collaborative devices in what concerns learning. It is important to underline that the comparison of individual and collaborative learning devices, central to most studies, can be discussed. Indeed, the activities in which the members of a group engage, whether it concerns the co-ordination or the management of the relationship and mutual comprehension, are very different from those of individual learning devices (M. Baker, 1994). It appears more heuristic to compare several collaborative devices differentiated by the resources they offer. This is what we propose in the present study, by opposing a complete collaborative writing device, in which the subjects dialogue and write an essay together, to a partial collaborative writing device, in which the subjects write an individual essay after having discussed together.

PROBLEMATICS

The present study proposes to analyse the forms of co-operation within a peer group in a learning through texts device, in order to identify the most productive ones, from the point of view of future acquisitions, and considering several levels: that of the collaborative devices—complete vs. partial; that of the working groups; and that of the participants.

This present work follows a preceding study that had compared, for this same task, an individual drafting device and a collaborative drafting device, the latter having appeared less effective from the point of view of learning (Olry-Louis, 2005). As it gives the script writer the possibility of organizing his own speech based on a certain point of view, individual drafting constitutes a specific thinking instrument. It thus probably does not play, from this point of view, the same cognitive role as collaborative drafting. According to us, a partially collaborative device, which would leave the subjects the possibility of discussion while obliging them to assimilate information in order to write an individual synthesis, should result in better training than the completely collaborative device, which deprives the subjects of the occasion of constructing their own individual written essay.

Rather than considering the collaborative devices as external learning factors, it seems important to clarify the social and cognitive mechanisms that underlie them. Therefore, we will seek to locate in the verbal exchanges how the cognitive constructions are built in each device and each small work group. In this perspective, particular attention will be given to the roles played by each individual, defined in speech analysis as "the various statement positions that a talking subject can take ... allowing definition of the communication activity of each participant" (Charaudeau & Main-gueneau, 2002, p. 514). For example, the subjects who ask numerous questions can be characterized by their interrogative role, those who give orders by their directing role. This more exploratory part will be guided by the data rather than by specific assumptions.

METHODOLOGY

Procedure

The experimentation took place in three phases. The first phase, focused on the pre-tests, gave the possibility to affect equivalent subjects under the various training conditions, on the basis of several tests presented elsewhere in detail (see Olry-Louis, 2005). The second phase consisted in applying the same learning through texts task to the subjects who had to make a written synthesis of a documentary file. The third phase took place three days later, without the participants being informed in advance, through an individual questionnaire to evaluate the quality of the acquisitions.

Participants

Sixty-two high-school students—33 females and 29 males of average age 16 years and 6 months—took part in the experiment. During the task, 32 participants wrote a collaborative essay—*complete collaboration*—and 30 others produced an individual essay after a phase of discussion—*partial collaboration*.

Once the high-school students were distributed in each device, we let them freely constitute small groups of four, several studies having shown that affinities play an important role in the quality of the exchanges and the cognitive benefit made (Murphy & Faulkner, 2000).

From this sample, which allowed the collection of quantitative data, a subsample was extracted, composed of 24 high-school students filmed during the task in order to make a qualitative analysis. This subsample was composed of 6 groups of 4 pupils, three of them coming from the *completely collaborative device*, the other three from the *partially collaborative device*.

The learning task

A set of documents was provided on a given geographical topic, "*Venice, its current problems, its future prospects*", showing the origins of the problem, the actor's points of view, and the stakes concerning the future decisions. The 14 documents in this file were taken from various sources (press, specialized magazines, tourist guides). After having read the documents and discussed the ideas in their group, the students had 2 hours to produce an individual (*partially collaborative device*) or a collective (*completely collaborative device*) synthesis of this file.

Observation tools

The evaluation of the productions

The syntheses produced by the pupils were analysed from the point of view of the argumentation by means of double marking, which allowed the calculation of concordance indices. With reference to the studies that differentiate the writings from experts and beginners in social sciences (E. L. Baker, 1994; Voss et al., 1983) several independent indicators were taken into account:

1. *Restored information* (RI) evaluates the quantity of information considered as important restored in the synthesis;
2. *Conceptual framework* (CF) evaluates the global explanatory dimension of the text, by taking into account the misinterpretations and the connectors or the verbs expressing causal relations;
3. *Speech organization* (SO) evaluates the level of integration presented in the plan;
4. *Geographical localizations* (GL) combine three indicators: suitable localizations, quantifications, and geographical terms; and
5. *Highlighting of controversies* (CO), each dissension between the actors and each paradox is underlined in the file being evaluated.

For these indicators, the value of the concordance coefficients was .97, .91, .80, .98, and .91, respectively.

A questionnaire was elaborated in order to evaluate the acquisitions. Half the questions concerned conceptual aspects evoked by several documents (comparisons, generalizations, inferences, personal standpoints, causal relations) and the other half concerned factual aspects (names of places or people, objects, numbers, dramatic details) evaluated through multiple-choice questions.

Analysis of how the participants operate in the devices and the small groups

In order to try to describe the variability of social and cognitive operations according to the devices, the participants and the small work groups, we used two coding grids referring to different levels of analysis, which we will present successively.

In order to compare the collaborative activity of the participants according to the devices, the coding of the exchanges in speech acts was carried out (grid 1). According to Chabrol and Bromberg (1999), the speech acts constitute, for the social actors, interactive means to solve concrete problems or symbolic systems, to co-construct a social reality. The set primitive categories called "spheres", proposed by these authors, try to account for what we jointly determine when we communicate:

- *the information sphere* relates to any act aiming at describing objects from the world in a non-evaluative way (to bring information, to question the veracity of the information . . .);
- *the evaluative sphere* relates to any act that formulates a judgement about the objects and the state of the world (to appreciate the conformity to a standard);
- *the interaction sphere* relates to any linguistic act aiming at co-constructing the partners' identities (to question a standpoint . . .);
- *the action sphere* relates to any act aiming at pushing to make something (to present an action as having to be accomplished in the future); and
- *the contract sphere* relates to any act that aims at regulating communication with reference to the goals and stakes (to manage the "what to do and how" or the "what to say, what to write, and how").

In order to differentiate the modes of co-operation on an individual level, in terms of roles and on the level of groups, in terms of interactive operations, a second analysis grid was applied to all the data collected (see Olry-Louis & Soidet, 2003, for more details). With a more detailed analysis grid, it is centred on the ten following types of intervention:

1. *Centration* (CENT): to focus the conversation on the task.
2. *Work impulse* (WI): to organize the work.
3. *Work control* (WC): to check the work and the behaviour of the others.
4. *Addition ideas* (AI): to put forward a new idea.
5. *Repetition* (REP): to repeat or reformulate an idea that has already been put forward.
6. *Request control of one's own comprehension* (RCC): to question the group in order to check that one has understood.
7. *Request argumentation* (RA): to ask another person to explain his ideas more precisely.
8. *Argumentation* (ARG): to give evidence, explanations.
9. *Dissension* (DIS): negative validation of the other's speech.
10. *Agreement* (AGR): positive validation of the other's speech.

The interventions of each subject in each group were coded and entered in the *sum of interventions* (SI) for each subject. One can thus study, on the basis of correlation analysis, the links between these variables and the performances variables. One can also observe interaction roles by means of a factorial analysis of the correspondences carried out on the interventions and the subjects.

This same analysis grid allows, by summation of the types of intervention, the description of the interactive operation of the small work groups. Each group is characterized by:

- *its interactive intensity* (total number of interventions emitted by the group);
- *the number of active participants* (participants producing 25% or more of the interventions of the group); and
- *the number of participants who were implicated in the task* (participants who did not produce digressions).

These indicators constitute the effectiveness criteria used to predict future performances. A forecast of maximum success is given when the group is characterized by an intense interaction and when each member of the group is active and implicated.

RESULTS

Compared effectiveness of the collaborative devices

Table 1 recapitulates all the variables taken into account under the two collaboration conditions in order to evaluate the quality of the syntheses

TABLE 1
Means and standard deviations of the variables evaluating the synthesis and the questionnaire

Variables	Partial collaboration		Complete collaboration	
	M	SD	M	SD
Restored information (RI)	3.75	1.41	4.39	1.26
Conceptual framework (CF)	4.80	2.97	5.73	2.61
Speech organization (SO)	1.73	0.73	1.97	0.82
Geographical localizations (GL)	4.18	1.74	5.53	1.15
Controversies (CO)	0.93	0.98	0.72	0.63
Score for the synthesis	15.40	6.41	18.34	5.39
Score for the questionnaire	10.53	3.03	10.66	3.98

produced during the task and the quality of the acquisitions evaluated by the questionnaire. For the synthesis, the two groups obtained comparable results for the Conceptual Framework, $t(60) = 1.32$, $p < .192$, the Speech Organization, $t(60) = 1.18$, $p < .242$, the Controversies, $t(60) = 1.03$, $p < .307$. But for the Restored Information, $t(60) = 1.89$, $p < .06$, the Geographical Localizations, $t(60) = 1.96$, $p < .05$, and the overall quality of the synthesis, $t(60) = 1.95$, $p < .05$, the participants placed in the completely collaborative condition obtained better results than those in the partially collaboration condition. However, the two groups showed no significant difference for the questionnaire, $t(60) = 0.15$, $p < .881$. Thus, the assumption according to which the individual drafting part characterizing the partially collaborative condition would be favourable to learning cannot be validated.

Activity implemented in the collaborative devices

On the basis of analysis grid 1, the 6 corpora collected were coded in 3505 speech acts, 2535 of which are produced in *complete collaboration* and 970 in *partial collaboration*. On the whole (Table 2), 32% of the exchanges concern the informative sphere, 28% are related to the interactive sphere, 20% to the contractual sphere, 13% to the action sphere, and 7% to the evaluation sphere.

What globally distinguishes the two collaborative conditions relates to the spheres of information, contract, and evaluation: the participants exchanged more with reference to the information sphere in the *complete collaboration* condition, and they related more to the evaluative and contract sphere in the *partial collaboration* condition. In addition, if we take into account the dimension of time, by distinguishing the distribution of the spheres in the first half of the exchanges and in the second half, we can see that the latter differentiates the two conditions: the *partial collaboration* groups reduced the remarks related to information and increased those

TABLE 2
Distribution, by interaction time, of the spheres in the two devices

	Complete collaboration			Partial collaboration			
	Time1	*Time2*	*Total*	*Time1*	*Time2*	*Total*	*Average*
Information	33,4	34,10	*33,70*	33,00	24,50	*28,90*	*32,40*
Evaluation	05,0	07,60	*06,30*	06,20	10,40	*08,20*	*06,80*
Interaction	25,90	29,60	*27,70*	25,80	29,00	*27,30*	*27,60*
Action	13,90	11,20	*12,60*	10,70	15,20	*12,90*	*12,70*
Contract	21,80	17,50	*19,70*	24,30	20,90	*22,70*	*20,00*

related to action and evaluation, whereas the *complete collaboration* groups at the end of the task limited the exchanges on action and contract.

Thus, initially, the subjects focused on the informative aspects and install the framework for their task. What differentiates the two conditions here is the greater importance given to the contract in the case of *partial collaboration* groups, as if those who were going to be separated for the writing phase felt a greater need to establish quickly the operational rules of the group, which each one would be able to integrate into later on. Correlatively, the volume of exchanges related to action appears more important in the case of *complete collaboration* groups, which seem to seize upon the common production target that was given to them.

In the second part of the exchanges, the linguistic activity changes in a major way for the *partial collaboration* groups. They forsake an important part of the informative sphere (the sphere that most characterizes the synthesis task) and give more room for the evaluation, action, and contract spheres, as if each person was in charge of the informative part in his personal draft, and the group had to build something else starting from there.

Types of intervention and interactional roles

With a more detailed analysis, the verbal interventions coded with grid 2 allowed, by the attribution of individual scores for each type of intervention, the characterization of the participants. We present successively the correlation analysis of these variables and the factorial analysis of the correspondences, which is based on the participants' profiles.

As Table 3 shows, the interventions most represented are Dissension (DIS), Agreement (AGR), and Information Addition (AI), with important inter-individual variations.

TABLE 3
Means and standard deviations of interventions types

Variables	M	S
Addition of ideas (AI)	15.58	14.78
Requested argumentation (RA)	5.29	3.45
Argumentation (ARG)	12.16	13.10
Work impulse (WI)	12.00	7.76
Control (CT)	9.62	10.34
Centration (CENT)	3.54	2.62
Dissension (DIS)	19.66	16.27
Agreement (AGR)	18.70	12.75
Repetition (REP)	12.08	13.66
Requested control of one's comprehension (RCC)	2.75	2.89
Total score of interventions (SI)	111.42	76.81

Table 4 accounts for the relations between the various types of interventions and with the performance variables. As the high level of correlations shows, the majority of the interventions were closely linked, except for the Requested Argumentation (RA), the Argumentation (ARG) and, to a lesser extent, the Centration (CENT), which appeared slightly or negatively correlated with the performance variables. The variables of Information (AI), Dissension (DIS), Agreement (AGR), Repetition (REP) and Request control of one's comprehension (RCC) had a significant positive relationship with the synthesis. Moreover, RCC was positively correlated to a significant degree with the acquisitions questionnaire. It should be noted that the two performance variables (synthesis and questionnaire) were slightly correlated.

The correlation of the total score of interventions (IS) by subject, all types considered, with the questionnaire is equal to zero, contrary to that with the synthesis, which is positive. However, this relation between the score of interventions and the synthesis varies according to the device considered: it is negative ($R = -.34$, $p < .30$) in partial collaboration and positive ($R = .72$, $p < .01$) in complete collaboration.

In order to reveal various *interactional roles*, the relations between the 10 types of interventions and the 24 participants were examined based on a factorial analysis of correspondences (see Figure 1). A first factorial axis, explaining 38% of the variance, opposes the Argumentation (ARG) and certain subjects on the positive pole, with the Control (CT) and other subjects on the negative pole. It is interpreted as a participation mode directed either towards the personal explanation by means of arguments, or towards the control of what is said or done by the others. The second factorial axis, explaining 22% of the variance, opposes the Requested Argumentation (RA) and the Centration (CENT) to the Addition of Ideas (AI) and to the Repetition (REP). We interpret this axis as linked to the attitude towards the task, sometimes interrogative, sometimes productive by the means of new ideas. On the basis of the positioning of the types of interventions and subjects on these two axes, interactional roles were defined. The *argumentator* qualifies the 4 pupils who seek to explain their position, as opposed to the role of *manager*, which characterizes the 4 pupils who control the others. *The questioner* role describes the attitude of the 5 pupils who find access to the contents of the task by asking questions, as opposed to the *constructive* role, specific to the 3 pupils centred on the production of ideas to work out the synthesis. The 8 subjects little represented in this graph were qualified as "*mixed*".

Interactive operationalization of the groups, success forecast and learning

Table 5 recapitulates all the results: the roles on an individual level, the indicators from grid 2 (interactive intensity, activity, and implication) on the

TABLE 4
Pearson correlation coefficients between interventions types, synthesis, and questionnaire

Variables	2	3	4	5	6	7	8	9	10	11	12	13
1. CENT	.20	.18	.24	.28	.21	.17	.28	.20	.20	.30	−.35	−.17
2. RA	–	.52**	.08	.28	.18	.22	.32	.13	.26	.35	−.02	−.26
3. ARG		–	.46*	.26	−.05	.35	.42*	.20	.23	.50*	.04	−.23
4. AI			–	.64***	.48**	.76***	.86***	.86***	.70***	.89***	.49*	.21
5. WI				–	80***	.67***	.77***	.77***	.60**	.83***	.21	.06
6. CT					–	.70***	.60**	.75***	.51**	.72***	.28	−.03
7. DIS						–	.82***	.86***	.61***	.90***	.55**	−.09
8. AGR							–	.83***	.67***	.93***	.43*	−.10
9. REP								–	.80***	.92***	.55**	.19
10. RCC									–	.74***	.52**	.41*
11. IS										–	.46*	.01
12. Synthesis											–	.27
13. Questionnaire												–

Notes: *p < .05; **p < .01; ***p < .001.

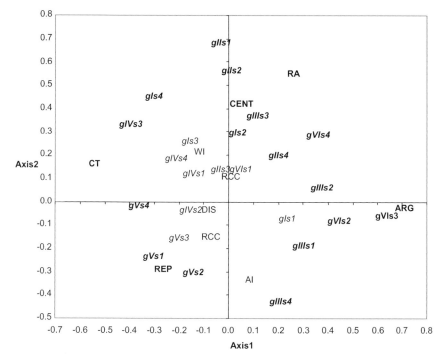

Figure 1. Factorial graph of correspondences (plan 1–2). *Types of intervention*: Centration (CENT), Work Impulse (WI), Control of work (CT), Addition of Ideas (AI), Repetition (REP), Requested control of one's own comprehension (RCC), Requested Argumentation (RA), Argumentation (ARG), Dissension (DIS), Agreement (AGR). *Individuals*: each subject is identified by his/her membership group (gI, gII, gIII, gIV, gV or gVI) and by his/her number in this group (s1, s2, s3 or s4). Only the subjects and interventions well represented in the plan are in bold.

level of the group, the real performances obtained during the written synthesis on the one hand, and of the questionnaire on the other hand, each one having been classified in 3 categories with equal numbers of persons ("weak", "average", "high"). On the basis of the qualitative data, forecasts were emitted (good, average, or poor success), which will be confronted by the real performances.

Let us examine initially the interactional roles. Although they were not considered for the forecasts, two of them deserve detailed attention as a result of their relationships to the performances on the questionnaire. The *constructive* role, which consists in providing ideas for the synthesis, proves to increase learning for the 3 participants that it characterizes. Conversely, the *questioner* role, characterized by Requested Argumentation and Centring, led to weak individual performances for 3 of the 5 participants so qualified.

TABLE 5
Synthesis of the observations and the performances by group

Group	Grid 2	Forecast	Perfo. synthesis	Perfo. question
I				
- 266 interventions	Mixed	High	High	High
- 3 actives	Questioner		High	High
- 4 implicated	Mixed		Average	Weak
	Manager		Average	Average
II				
- 211 interventions	Questioner	Weak	Weak	Weak
- 2 actives	Questioner		Weak	Average
- 3 implicated	Mixed		Weak	High
	Argumentator		Average	Average
III				
- 400 interventions	Constructive	Average	High	High
- 2 actives	Argumentator		Weak	Average
- 4 implicated	Questioner		Average	Weak
	Constructive		High	High
IV				
- 386 interventions	Mixed	Weak	Weak	Weak
- 3 actives	Mixed			Weak
- 0 implicated	Manager			Weak
	Mixed			High
V				
- 964 interventions	Manager	High	High	High
- 4 actives	Constructive			High
- 4 implicated	Mixed			Average
	Manager			High
VI				
- 447 interventions	Mixed	Average	Average	Average
- 2 actives	Argumentator			Weak
- 4 implicated	Argumentator			Average
	Questioner			High

While examining each group according to its level of success forecast, we will now attach ourselves to the indicators of interactive operation in group.

Two groups had a good success forecast. Group V had an optimal way of working, considering the model adopted. All the participants were implicated and active; the interaction was intense. Indeed, with the questionnaire and the synthesis, the participants obtained good performances for 3 of them. For group I, the forecast of high success, given because of the implication and activity ratios, was confirmed, although one participant (gIs3) remained rather passive during the interactions, obtaining lower performances than those envisaged.

For two other groups, the forecast was that of poor success because of weak activity, interaction, and implication ratios. This was the case in group II, characterized by minimal activity and interactions. If the performances at the synthesis were compatible with this forecast, those obtained with the questionnaire were higher than those expected. The poor operational work of the group seems to have compromised individual acquisitions less than collaborative work. For group IV, for which a weak success forecast had been given following a set of negative indices, in particular an absence of implication, the results confirmed the assumption, except for one participant, who was more withdrawn during the exchanges related to digressions.

The last two groups prompted a forecast of average success considering the heterogeneous indicators. For groups III and VI, certain positive criteria (the implication) indeed coexisted with negative criteria (weak activity and average intensity). The results of the synthesis and the questionnaire, globally averaged, were also heterogeneous.

As a whole, the success forecasts given were equivalent in both collaboration devices. What varied between the two was the reliability of the success predictions about the questionnaire: if in the *complete collaboration* device, the predictions were confirmed in 8 cases out of 12, they were only confirmed in 4 cases out of 12 for the *partial collaboration* device. The meaning of the variations of the prediction also changed: under the *complete collaboration* condition, 3 of the 4 forecast errors were due to an over estimation of the performances, under the *partial collaboration* condition, 5 of the 8 forecast errors were linked to under valuations. The forecasts emitted being based only on what was observed during the interactions, it is clear that the individual part of the *partial collaboration* condition, devoted to the writing of a text, perceptibly modulated the effects of the interactive mode, and generally in a way that was favourable to acquisitions.

DISCUSSION

Which are the most productive types of co-operation?

The emitted predictions have a suitable reliability when the way in which the group operates constitutes the object of the analysis, although it varies according to the weight given to the four criteria considered. Considering the results, one criterion weighs more than the others. It is the implication of all in the task that, when it is absent from the observations made on the group, leads to weak future performances whatever the values of the other criteria. It thus has the status of necessary criterion, but not sufficient. The value of the forecast of the two other criteria—interactive intensity and the activity of all the members—confirms the data from the literature (Cohen, 1994; Mulryan, 1992). Furthermore, it is important to underline that with these indicators of the way in which the groups operate, one predicts more surely the quality of the written production at the end of the discussion than the quality of each member's acquisitions, which suggests that the mental activity of the participants is not limited to their remarks.

When the subjects were taken as analysis units, we observed that the quality of the synthesis was related to the volume of interventions (cf. Cohen, 1994), certain types of interventions being particularly determinant, whether it concerns addition of ideas, agreement, dissension, repetition, or control of one's own comprehension. Only the latter contributes, however, to the quality of learning; it is obviously related to the metacognitive aspects described in the literature (Hayes, 1996).

We also noticed that the second axis of the factorial analysis of the correspondences, which provides the possibility of opposing the questioner role with the constructive role, is also indirectly related to distinct levels of learning, weak for the first, high for the second. Considering the nature of the task, it is possible to conceive that the constructive role, characterized by the production of ideas to work out the synthesis, is associated with success. This role appears to be the one most centred on the elements of the contents. It is thus relevant for the integration of the elements in a set of information as well as for the memorizing of the data contained in the documents. What the subjects called "questioners" seem to have lacked is, first, the opportunity to produce the contents by themselves in order to memorize them and, second, actively to use the answers they obtained when they asked questions (Webb et al., 1995).

What is the social and cognitive impact of the collaboration devices?

We initially supposed that the *partial collaborative drafting device*, by forcing the subjects to construct an individual written answer, would be very efficient because it combines the confrontation of ideas with other persons and the individual reappropriation of knowledge. What did we learn about this point?

When we compare, on a quantitative level, the average performances obtained under the two conditions, the written productions appear to be less elaborated in this device, whereas the quality of acquisitions, equivalent under the two conditions, is not affected.

The analysis of the speech acts showed that, on the one hand, in the partial collaboration device, the volume of exchanges was two and a half times weaker, and, on the other hand, the speech activity changed during the task, as if there were a rupture in the task and in the group at the same time: the information evocation, essential to elaborate a synthesis, becomes gradually less present, while the room left for evaluation and the contract increases. We can imagine that they would have worked in a different way if the pressure of time had been less present, since, as we pointed out previously, the participants had a total of 2 hours to read, discuss, and write an essay. We can also evoke the fact that engagement is less important in the group because, in the end, the production is individual. On this point it is important to underline that, in complete collaboration, the greater the volume of exchanges, the more the quality of the collective essay benefits. In partial collaboration, this relation could not be established, as if the quality of the written productions depended less on the interactive way of working that was adopted during the discussion than on a more individual way of working.

The reliability of our predictions also depends on the device considered: it is when the activity of writing the text is collective—complete collaboration—that individual acquisitions are best predicted. When the writing is individual, the performances evaluated, which are very heterogeneous, are mostly higher than those expected. This suggests that partial collaboration facilitates the personal reconstruction of what was discussed in the group.

In a general way, the analysis showed that certain participants, once placed in small groups, continue to work on an individual level using their own resources—nothing prevents them from that because the documents remain visible. It is all the more true as the group proves to be quite unproductive and, besides, the device in which they are placed highlights the individual production, which is the case for the *partial collaboration* device.

To finish, we would like to underline with others (Buchs, Butera, & Mugny, 2004; Johnson et al., 1990) the importance of research on co-operation devices, in particular according to whether or not they give the participants the possibility to operate individually. According to us, in order to make it possible for such research to be as fruitful as possible, it should seek to use jointly quantitative and qualitative methods, the latter being capable of clarifying the results of the former.

REFERENCES

Arvaja, M., Häkkinen, P., Eteläpelto, A., & Rasku-Puttonen, H. (2000). Collaborative processes during report writing of a science learning project: The nature of discourse as a function of task requirements. *European Journal of Psychology of Education, 15,* 455–466.

Baker, E. L. (1994). Learning-based assessments of history understanding. *Educational Psychologist, 29,* 97–106.

Baker, M. (1994). A model for negotiation in teaching–learning dialogues. *Journal of Artificial Intelligence in Education, 5,* 199–124.

Baker, M., Brixhe, D., & Quignard, M. (2002). La co-élaboration des notions scientifiques dans les dialogues entre apprenants: Le cas des interactions médiatisées par ordinateur. In J. Bernicot, A. Trognon, M. Guidetti, & M. Musiol (Eds.), *Pragmatique et psychologie* (pp. 109–138). Nancy, France: Presses Universitaires de Nancy.

Braaksma, M. A. H., Rijlardaam, G., van den Berg, H., & Van Hout-Wolters, B. H. A. M. (2004). Observational learning and its effects on the orchestration of writing processes. *Cognition and Instruction, 22,* 1–36.

Britt, M. A., & Aglinskas, C. (2002). Improving students ability to identify and use source information. *Cognition and Instruction, 20,* 485–522.

Brixhe, D., Marro-Clément, P., & Picard, A. F. (1996). Gestion interactive de séquences explicatives. *Interaction et cognitions, 2–3,* 425–456.

Bruner, J. S. (1983). *Le développement de l'enfant: savoir faire, savoir dire.* Paris: Presses Universitaires de France.

Buchs, C., Butera, F., & Mugny, G. (2004). Resource independence, student interactions, and performance in cooperative learning. *Educational Psychology, 24,* 291–314.

Carretero, M., & Voss, J. F. (Eds.). (1994). *Cognitive and instructional processes in history and the social sciences.* Hillsdale, NJ: Lawrence Erlbaum Associates, Inc.

Chabrol, C., & Bromberg, M. (1999). Préalables à une classification des actes de parole. *Psychologie française, 44,* 291–306.

Charaudeau, P., & Maingueneau, D. (2002). *Dictionnaire d'analyse du discours.* Paris: Seuil.

Chi, M. T. H., Siler, S. A., & Jeong, H. (2004). Can tutors monitor students' understanding accurately? *Cognition and Instruction, 22,* 363–387.

Cohen, E. G. (1994). Restructuring the classroom: Conditions for productive small groups. *Review of Educational Research, 64,* 1–35.

Crook, C. (1995). On resourcing a concern for collaboration within peer interactions. *Cognition and Instruction, 13,* 541–547.

Doise, W., & Mugny, G. (1997). *Psychologie sociale du développement cognitif* (2nd ed.). Paris: Armand Colin.

Fayol, M. (1997). *Des idées au texte—Psychologie cognitive de la production verbale, orale et écrite.* Paris: Presses universitaires de France.

Gillies, R. M. (2004). The effects of cooperative learning on junior high school students during small group learning. *Learning and Instruction, 14,* 197–213.

Gillies, R. M., & Ashman, A. F. (1996). Teaching collaborative skills to primary school children in classroom-based work groups. *Learning and Instruction, 6,* 187–200.

Gillies, R. M., & Ashman, A. F. (1998). Behavior and interactions of children in cooperative groups in lower and middle elementary grades. *Journal of Educational Psychology, 90,* 746–757.

Gilly, M., Fraisse, J., & Roux, J. P. (1988). Résolution de problèmes en dyades et progrès cognitifs chez des enfants de 11 à 13 ans. In A. N. Perret-Clermont & M. Nicolet (Eds.), *Interagir et connaître. Enjeux et régulations sociales dans le développement cognitif* (pp. 73–92). Cousset, France: Delval.

Gilly, M., Roux, J. P., & Trognon, A. (Eds.). (1999). *Apprendre dans l'interaction.* Nancy, France: Presses Universitaires de Nancy; Aix-En-Provence: Publications de l'université de Provence.

Graesser, A. C., Person, N. K., & Magliano, J. P. (1995). Collaborative dialogue patterns in naturalistic one-to-one tutoring. *Applied Cognitive Psychology, 9,* 495–522.

Greene, S. (1994). The problems of learning to think like a historian: Writing history in the culture of the classroom. *Educational Psychologist, 29,* 89–96.

Grosjean, M., & Traverso, V. (2002). Les polylogues: Typologie, problèmes méthodologiques et théoriques. *Psychologie de l'interaction, 15–16,* 283–303.

Grossen, M. (1994). Theoretical and methodological consequences of a change in the unit of analysis for the study of peer interactions in a problem solving situation. *European Journal of Psychology of Education, 9,* 159–173.

Grossen, M., & Bachmann, K. (2000). Learning to collaborate in a peer-tutoring situation: Who learns? What is learned? *European Journal of Psychology of Education, 15*, 491–508.

Hayes, J. R. (1996). A new framework for understanding cognition and affect in writing. In C. M. Levy & S. E. Ransdell (Eds.), *The science of writing. Theories, methods, individual differences and applications* (pp. 1–27). Mahwah, NJ: Lawrence Erlbaum Associates, Inc.

Hoyles, C., & Forman, E. A. (1995). Introduction at special issue: Processes and products of collaborative problem solving, some interdisciplinary perspectives. *Cognition and Instruction, 13*, 479–482.

Johnson, D. W., Johnson, R. T., Stanne, M. B., & Garibaldi, A. (1990). Impact of group processing on achievement in cooperative groups. *The Journal of Social Psychology, 130*, 507–516.

Joiner, R., Littleton, K., Faulkner, D., & Miell, D. (Eds.). (2000). *Rethinking collaborative learning*. London: Free Association Press.

King, A., Staffieri, A., & Adelgais, A. (1998). Mutual peer tutoring: Effects of structuring tutorial interaction to scaffold peer learning. *Journal of Educational Psychology, 90*, 134–152.

Kintsch, W. (1988). The use of knowledge in discourse processing: A construction–integration model. *Psychological Review, 95*, 163–182.

Kuhn, D., Shaw, V., & Felton, M. (1997). Effects of dyadic interaction on argumentative reasoning. *Cognition and Instruction, 15*, 287–315.

Kumpalainen, K., & Mutanen, M. (1999). The situated dynamics of peer group interaction: An introduction to an analytic framework. *Learning and instruction, 9*, 449–473.

McNamara, D. S., Kintsch, E., Butler Songer, N., & Kintsch, W. (1996). Are good texts always better? Interactions of text coherence, background knowledge, and levels of understanding in learning from text. *Cognition and Instruction, 14*, 1–43.

Mercer, N. (1996). The quality of talk in children's collaborative activity in the classroom. *Learning and Instruction, 6*, 359–377.

Mulryan, C. M. (1992). Student passivity during cooperative small groups in mathematics. *Journal of Educational Research, 85*, 261–273.

Murphy, S., & Faulkner, D. (2000). Learning to collaborate: Can young children develop better communication strategies through collaboration with a more popular peer. *European Journal of Psychology of Education, 15*, 389–404.

Olry-Louis, I. (2003). Coopérer et apprendre par le dialogue—Enjeux et perspectives. *L'Orientation Scolaire et Professionnelle, 32*, 343–358.

Olry-Louis, I. (2005). Co-construire des connaissances à partir de textes. *Psychologie de l'Interaction, 19–20*, 99–156.

Olry-Louis, I., & Soidet, I. (2003). Coopérer pour co-construire des savoirs: Une approche différentielle. *L'orientation Scolaire et Professionnelle, 32*, 503–535.

Perret-Clermont, A. N. (1996). *La construction de l'intelligence dans l'interaction sociale* (2nd ed.). Berne, Switzerland: Peter Lang.

Rouet, J. F., Britt, M. A., Mason, R. A., & Perfetti, C. A. (1996). Using multiple sources of evidence to study historical controversies. *Journal of Educational Psychology, 88*, 476–493.

Roussey, J. Y., Farioli, F., & Piolat, A. (1992). Effects of social regulation and computer assistance on the monitoring of writing. *European Journal of Psychology of Education, 7*, 295–309.

Scardamalia, M., & Bereiter, C. (1991). Literate expertise. In K. A. Ericsson & J. Smith (Eds.), *Toward a general theory of expertise* (pp. 172–194). Cambridge, UK: Cambridge University Press.

Shachar, H., & Sharan, S. (1994). Talking, relating and achieving—Effects of cooperative learning and whole-class instruction. *Cognition and Instruction, 12*, 313–353.

Sorsana, C. (2003). Comment l'interaction coopérative rend-elle plus savant? Quelques réflexions concernant les conditions nécessaires au fonctionnement dialogique du conflit socio-cognitif? *L'Orientation Scolaire et Professionnelle, 32*, 437–473.

Teasley, S. D. (1995). The role of talk in children's peer collaborations. *Developmental Psychology, 31*, 207–220.

Trognon, A., & Batt, M. (2003). Comment représenter le passage de l'Intersubjectif à l'Intrasubjectif? Essai de Logique Interlocutoire. *L'Orientation Scolaire et Professionnelle, 32*, 399–436.

Van Dijk, T. A., & Kintsch, W. (1983). *Strategies of discourse comprehension.* New York: Academic Press.

Voss, J. F., Greene, T. R., Post, T. A., & Penner, B. C. (1983). Problem-solving in the social sciences. *The Psychology of Learning and Motivation, 17*, 165–213.

Voss, J. F., & Ney Silfies, L. (1996). Learning from history text: The interaction of knowledge and comprehension skill with text structure. *Cognition and Instruction, 43*, 45–68.

Vygotsky, L. S. (1985). *Pensée et langage.* Paris: Editions Sociales. (Originally published 1934).

Webb, N. M. (1989). Peer interaction and learning in small groups. *International Journal of Educational Research, 13*, 21–39.

Webb, N. M., & Mastergeorge, A. M. (2003). The development of students' helping behavior and learning in peer-directed small groups. *Cognition and Instruction, 21*, 361–428.

Webb, N. M., Troper, J. D., & Fall, R. (1995). Constructive activity and learning in collaborative small groups. *Journal of Educational Psychology, 87*, 406–423.

Wiley, J., & Voss, J. F. (1999). Constructing arguments from multiples sources: Tasks that promote understanding and not just memory for text. *Journal of Educational Psychology, 91*, 301–311.

Wineburg, S. S. (1991). Historical problem solving: A study of the cognitive process used in the evaluation of documentary and pictorial evidence. *Journal of Educational Psychology, 83*, 73–87.

Zammuner, V. L. (1995). Individual and cooperative computer writing and revising: Who gets the best results? *Learning and Instruction, 5*, 101–124.

EUROPEAN JOURNAL OF DEVELOPMENTAL PSYCHOLOGY
2008, 5 (5), 609–622

An interlocutory analysis as a methodological approach in studying cognitivo-linguistic mediations: Interest, difficulties, and limits

Jean-Paul Roux

IUFM of Aix-Marseille and PsyCLE Research Centre, University of Provence, Aix-en-Provence, France

According to a Vygotskian approach, apprenticeship and cognitive development are linked with the internalization of significant function of language signs, namely with the ability to use words as conceptual tools. Such an internalization is not possible without social mediation and meaning negotiation, within (or consecutively to) an interactive situation. Because within this socio-cognitive process (both inter-individual and intra-individual), linguistic signs play a principal role, a logical analysis of the interlocution seems to be a powerful way to study interlocutive processes: It permits us to understand how semiotic mediations can produce, via exchanged speech acts, new knowledge and new social and cognitive tools. However, we will evoke some theoretical and methodological problems encountered in interaction analysis with young children: the validity (i) of transcription of the reality (coding is transforming, more or less); (ii) of interdiscusive corpus analysed (How can we transcribe punctuation of discourses as well as affects and its perlocutory aims? Are chosen sequences relevant to be analysed?); and (iii) of the researcher's inferences regarding the effective mechanisms; the importance of nonverbal signs within a conversation; and the difficulty (i) of abstracting structures of transactions and (ii) of measuring both the impact of subject's previous social and cognitive experience and representations concerning the partner.

Keywords: Conversation; Interaction analysis; Interlocutory analysis; Social mediation; Speech acts.

INTRODUCTION

The epistemological position we have adopted regarding cognitive processes, according to the socio-constructivist Vygotskian principles,

Correspondence should be addressed to Jean Paul Roux, IUFM site d'Aix, 2 Avenue Jules Isaac, F – 13626 Aix-en-Provence Cedex 1. E-mail: jeanpaul.roux@free.fr

http://www.psypress.com/edp DOI: 10.1080/17405620801994922

postulates that the human cognition should be conceived as a consequence of the participation in interactions with others, thanks to semiotic mediations. So, we have to focus on the regulations between social exchanges and cognition in order to explain inter-psychological origins of intra-psychological cognitive functioning and development (Wertsch & Sanmarco, 1988).

Among the semiotic mediations, and in particular owing to the fact that the interlocutive reality of the linguistic communication is indubitable, the linguistic exchanges appear as most relevant (and thus most studied!). Indeed, conversation, essentially interactive, must be regarded as the place, simultaneously, of social relations and contents of thought. So, we absolutely need a theory of the interactive processes, to explain the structuring of the cognition of the partners.

The aim of this paper is to show not only the interest, but also the difficulties of the theory of interlocutory logic (Roux, 2001a, 2001b, 2003; Trognon, 1999, 2001; Trognon & Batt, 2003; Trognon & Kostulski, 1999) as a method of study of the cognitivo-linguistic exchanges.

THE VYGOTSKIAN MODEL OF THE SOCIAL ORIGIN OF HIGHER MENTAL PROCESSES: STATUS AND FUNCTION OF THE LANGUAGE WITHIN COMMUNICATIVE PROCESSES

Concerning our topic, from the socio-historical model of cognitive processes (Vygotsky, 1933/1985, 1934/1985), we can retain the three following main ideas. The first is that the functioning and the development of cognitive abilities are consequences of apprenticeship realized within interactive social processes mediated by signs. The second is that the apprenticeship and the cognitive development are linked with the internalization of significant function of the signs of the language (namely, with the ability to use words as conceptual tools). The third is that such an internalization is not possible without a social mediation and a negotiation of the meaning within (or consecutively to) an interlocutory context.

The cognitive evolution, as a consequence of the "from inter to intra" process, accomplished within (or after) social situations is not a product corresponding to an appropriation "from the same to the same" (Wertsch, 1985). It is always a rebuilding, thanks to the transformation of the communicative function of the signs into representative function. Indeed, every conversation is organized, thanks to *transactions* (i.e., thanks to socio-cognitive sequences aiming to *negotiate* and to *elaborate meaning*) towards the construction of intersubjectivity between the actors (Gilly, Roux, & Trognon, 1999). Signs exchanged, within such a dialogical context, assume *simultaneously* two essential functions: a *social* function (i.e., to communicate) and a *cognitive* function (i.e., to mean and to represent). Thus, the social and communicative function (*inter-psychic*) of the signs exchanged can become individual (*intra-psychic*) and intellectual cognitive tools, increasing the subject's ability to think by himself or herself (Bronckart, 1997, 2000).

Because interlocutory contexts are logically organized (Vanderveken, 1988, 1999, Vanderveken & Kubo, 2001) and because within socio-cognitive processes (both inter-individual and intra-individual), linguistic signs play a constructive role, one can think with Trognon (1999), on the one hand, that conversation is a matrix of achievement of both social and cognitive abilities and tools. On the other hand, we think that a pragmatic analysis of the interlocutory context is a powerful methodological way to study the cognitive functioning and development of interlocutors. So, a logical analysis of the interlocution allows us to understand how semiotic mediations can produce, via exchanged speech acts, both new knowledge and new social and cognitive tools for individuals.

THE THEORY OF THE INTERLOCUTORY LOGIC: A POWERFUL METHODOLOGICAL TOOL

Fundamental principles

This theory, elaborated by Trognon and his research team (Trognon, 1999, 2001, 2003), is an empirical approach elaborated with respect to conversational properties. Aiming to permit a pragmatic analysis of conversational sequences, this theory integrates different fields (linguistics, cognitive sciences, psychology, philosophy) and different theories (general semantics, speech act theory) regarding the conversation.

The theory of speech acts (see Armengaud, 1985/1993; Austin, 1962; Ghiglione & Trognon, 1993; Kerbrat-Orecchioni, 1990; Roulet, Auchlin, Moeschler, Rubattel, & Schelling, 1991; Searle & Vanderveken, 1985; Vanderveken, & Kubo, 2001) is based on a pragmatic study of linguistic enunciations emitted within verbal exchanges. In this theory, one postulate that the *performance* of the enunciation is a social act. Within an interaction, in any circumstance, to speak is to establish with others a more or less significant space, each verbal enunciation aiming at doing something. A speech act (Ghiglione & Trognon, 1993; Searle, 1969/1972; Vanderveken, 1988) is generally symbolized by F(p), or F(rp). F corresponds to the "*force*", concerning the socio-relational aspect of the action upon others and p (or rp) corresponds to the "*prepositional content*", concerning the cognitive aspects, that enunciate the state of things or the predicated action to be accomplished (Searle & Vanderveken, 1985).

According to Searle's proposal, one can distribute the speech acts among five main categories (the "grammar of acts") that concern the primitive illocutionary forces:

- *Assertives* concern the locutor's interest regarding the state of the world, engaging him/her and expressing his/her conviction about it.
- *Directives* (more or less directly) express the locutor's wish to obtain a behaviour from his/her interlocutor: the prepositional content remains always the accomplishment of an action, the force varying from the more imploring prayer to the more imperious edict.
- *Commissives* are directives explicitly addressed by locutors to themselves, to engage themselves towards a future action.
- *Declaratives* create a new world, just saying it is. This type of act creates a link between words and the world, i.e., between the prepositional content and the reality.
- *Expressives* express the locutor's frame of mind specified within the prepositional content, without adjustment between words and world.

Conversational negotiation processes are sequential and articulated according to logical links. To analyse these processes, two main properties of speech acts have to be taken into account: *success* (linked with the *non-defectivity*) and *satisfaction*. A speech act is *successful* when its aim is clearly recognized by the interactor, in other words, when the locutor succeeds (in a context of utterance) in pressing upon his/her partner the nature of his/her act (Ghiglione & Trognon, 1993; Vanderveken, 1988). A speech act is *satisfied* when the wished for perlocutory effect is obtained (i.e., when its prepositional content is effected within the enunciation context, regardless of its force).

Regarding the principle of *locality*, each illocution emitted by an interlocutor is a contextualized (or "situated") action. Regarding the principle of *over determination*, each conversational element is both a social event and a cognitive event, and it is impossible to separate these two aspects, each over determined. Finally, regarding the principle of *processuality*, the different elements of each conversation are elaborated progressively, step by step.

Within a conversation, as transactions are structured by exchanges, the *force* and the *propositional content* of speech acts of interlocutors are logically linked. So, one can think that analysing step by step the speech acts emitted within the conversation permits us to understand the organization of the socio-cognitive events and the underlying cognitive mechanisms within the interlocutory process (Marro-Clément, Trognon, & Perret-Clermont, 1999).

Regarding the above considerations, the theory of the interlocutory logic seems today a powerful tool to describe the interactions having apprenticeship for a goal and in understanding the effects of interactions on the cognition of interlocutors. In fact, the interest of this methodological tool is multiple. One can describe how social and cognitive features of verbal exchanges are structured and linked, and so it is possible to describe the nature of partners' representations, which are emerging from current negotiations. One can identify the co-construction of new representations or new conceptions (carried by propositional contents of speech acts), which are emerging from the conversation. One can visualize in real time how interlocutors agree in solving their problem; in brief, to confirm the thesis according to which "conversation and reasoning are constructed at the same time" (Trognon, Saint-Dizier de Almeida, & Grossen, 1999, p. 139). One can validate the researcher's interpretations: this is possible because the theory permits us to make inferences concerning the subject's knowledge (in terms of state or of developmental level) at each stage of the conversation in progress. And, finally, one can formulate a theoretical model for the emergence of cognitive competence.

The analysis of the interlocutory context: One example

We propose an illustration of how it is possible to describe and to understand teacher–pupil interactions within a didactical process (cf. Roux & Froment, 2004).

The situational context is the following. Within a pre-school classroom situational context, the teacher's didactical objectives are to elaborate in pupils (aged 4–5 years) the ability to organize (to classify) objects into a Cartesian table and to acculturate pupils (to elaborate "thinking forms"). Pupils are sitting around the material-support (i.e., different objects to classify and a Cartesian table).

This device expresses two teacher's conceptions about apprenticeship: the teacher has to create a context allowing in children the elaboration of a pragmatic schema, i.e., a socio-cognitive tool organized in two elements: a representative unit (to attribute a meaning to a task), and a resolution unit (to facilitate the success in this task); and the teacher has to manage situational, interactional and interlocutory contexts, directing the whole series of exchanges concerning "what it is necessary to do", and "which is the type of answer required".

The conversation between the teacher and the pupils (Table 1) reveals the understanding of the teacher's expectations by pupils, permitting them to build a sufficient degree of common meaning about the situation. This permits the learners to anticipate, concerning both the nature of the task, the expected behaviours and postures, and the attributed roles and social places.

TABLE 1

Succession of illocutions, analysis of the speech acts, and inferences concerning the state of the speaker's cognition throughout the conversation

Succession of illocutions	Speech acts	Conversational analysis (state of participant's cognition)	
		Force	Propositional content
1-Teacher-l: OK, what did I put on the ground?	Dir (material)	Asking general question regarding material	Teacher wants to start the pupil's cognitive activity by initiating an episode that returns to a "formatted" activity: pupils must "name" the material support and "clarify" the task
2-Some pupils: a carpet	Ass (carpet)	T1: R/S	Some: The material support is "a carpet"
3-Teacher-2a: a carpet!	Ass (carpet)	Some: R/S	Teacher ratifies the answer "carpet"
3-Teacher-2b: a carpet with flowers?	Dir (carpet detail)	She wants to have a more precise answer	But she is not totally satisfied. Thus, she asks for a detail regarding the material support
4-Some pupils: no :::::	Ass (carpet detail)	T-2: R/S	Some: The carpet does not have flowers
5-Sabine: with small squares	Ass (carpet detail)	T-2: R/S with an important detail	Sab: The carpet is composed of "small squares"
6-Teacher-3a: with small squares, OK	Ass (carpet detail)	Some: R/S	Teacher accepts "small squares" but is not completely satisfied
6-Teacher-3b: It's a :::	Dir (material)	Question	Waiting a specific answer (probably "squaring") she raises a question to obtain it ....
7-Karim: A squaring!	Ass (material=a squaring)	T-3a: R/S	Karim: The carpet (material with which one will work) represents a "squaring"

(continued)

TABLE 1
(Continued)

Succession of illocutions	Speech acts	Conversational analysis (state of participant's cognition)	
		Force	*Propositional content*
8-Teacher-4: OK, You are right, one calls that . . .	Ass (material=squaring)	Karim: R/S	The teacher ratifies Karim's answer defining the carpet as a "squaring" made up of "full of small boxes"
9-Lea: with blue and green features!	Ass (material=squaring)	Lea: T-4: R/S	Lea: The carpet represents a "squaring" with blue and green features

Notes: Dir=directive; Ass=assertive; R=success; S=satisfaction; :::=silence.

Thanks to these formatted situations, throughout the didactic dialogue the pupils are acculturated. Thanks to teacher's statements (overall through assertives and directives) and to teacher's explanations (guidance), pupils have the opportunity to learn social attitudes (e.g., how to behave with respect to a special type of social setting), socio-cognitive abilities (e.g., what are the principles of an answer), and cognitive and metacognitive tools (e.g., strategies and procedures). However, regarding the effects of this didactical method, some comments can be made.

Which kind of "pragmatic schema" do the children build (or have they built)? Thanks to the formatting interactional context, they can learn (but how to make sure that they learned everything?) to manage a Cartesian table. Indeed, routines are more or less ritualized practices that aim (explicitly or implicitly), on the one hand, to control the social situations and social interactions and, on the other hand, to share the activities and/or the cognition of the children. They thus play a double part: social (regulating effect on the behaviours); and cognitive (they are "formatted" organizers of the thought: representation of the goal and solving procedures).

The teacher wants to engage pupils by attracting their attention regarding new material. She manages the conversation through questions requiring more and more precision. She wants to make sure that the material elements, supports of the task, are known. Concerning this specific method of questioning, one can formulate three remarks:

1. She stimulates the pupil's cognitive activity by apparently open questions: in fact, the expected answers have to be precise and do not offer a real choice.
2. She does not question a specific pupil; anybody can answer: in fact, this gives the "good speakers" an advantage over the other pupils.
3. When a pupil provides the expected answer, she ratifies it and she continues her didactic dialogue, as if all the pupils had built a maximum degree of intersubjectivity with her: this is not certain.

SOME THEORETICAL AND METHODOLOGICAL PROBLEMS ENCOUNTERED IN INTERACTION ANALYSIS

These problems and limits, although essential, are not specific. But, as they arise each time we want to observe individuals in interaction to explain their effects by the understanding of the processes and the mechanisms involved, these limits have to be taken into account. Some of them are presented below, with some proposals to answer and/or to solve them.

General problems regarding the observation of social situations

Before any observation, the researcher has to solve the difficult problem of the validity of the whole of the device and, specifically, the relevance of the task(s) proposed.

Is the observation objective and relevant?   To observe a social situation is frequently to modify this situation regarding what generally happens in this kind of situation. First, and for a long time, it has been known that the presence of an observer and/or the technical tools he (or she) uses can modify the verbal and nonverbal behaviours of the actors. So, it is necessary to accustom the various actors to this presence (human and/or technical) to minimize its impact. Second, one must always pose the question regarding the relevance of the tools used: indeed, the validity of the collected corpora depends on the validity of them.

Are the selected and collected corpora and units relevant?   From the situational and the interactional context to the interlocutory context analysed many theoretical and methodological choices are necessary. These choices, concerning each scientific device, are always linked to the theoretical position, the aim(s) of the research and the hypothesis formulated. These are fundamental choices, because they determine the relevance of the subsequent analysis. So, some questions have to be asked: Are the chosen different contexts relevant? Within these contexts, are the selected corpora relevant? And are the units chosen relevant? To limit this difficulty, regarding the theoretical and methodological constructs, the researcher has to choose carefully the corpora and units to be analysed.

Specific problems regarding the analysis of an interlocutory context

After the periods of observation and collecting data, comes the time of the coding and analysis of these data. The problems we are faced with are the following:

Is the transcription valid?   Regardless of the fact that the transcription is very time consuming (at least one hour for one minute), to code behaviours into words is transforming the reality, more or less. The transcribed corpora are generally pale reflections of the reality! It is quite easy to transcribe illocutions clearly emitted by the partners of the interaction. But, in spite of the precision of the chosen criteria, and in spite of the respect of conventional rules established for the transcription, it is virtually impossible to transcribe into words all the events that happened within a conversation. In particular, it is always difficult (and often impossible) to transcribe "punctuation" of discourses (e.g., hesitations, silences, hubbubs, rhythms, prosodies), and to evaluate and transcribe the affects and their perlocutory aims. To reduce these problems, it is essential to transcribe as precisely as possible each illocution, noting associated nonverbal events and the different characteristics of the speech. A precaution is to test the transcribed corpora using a "judge method".

How to take into account and analyse the nonverbal behaviours?   Within a face-to-face conversation, nonverbal behaviours, attitudes, as well as affects are always present and play a role more or less important regarding the nature of both the situational and the interactional contexts. How to transcribe these nonverbal behaviours, attitudes, and affects? How to analyse their effect upon conversation? A pragmatic and powerful solution to surmount this obstacle (see Roux, 2001b), is to take into account the nonverbal acts and attitudes (of course, when it is possible!) as conventional illocutions and, taking them into account simultaneously with the partner reactions, to analyse them as speech acts (assertives, directives, etc.).

Are the researcher's inferences relevant?   Even if any conversation is logically organized, according to the principles of locality, over determination, and processuality (Trognon, 1999, 2001, 2003), it is not possible to allot a univocal origin and a univocal meaning to "distributed" cognitions of the partners, which are "located" *hic et nunc* in the particular "micro-world" of a transaction. Here, the main question is that of the "true" logic of the transaction. How to know what is the "true" logic? Is the researcher's inferred logic isomorphic with the logic of the interlocutors? Nevertheless, the researcher must make inferences about this logic, while knowing that the conclusions are always more or less risky and/or limited. And, obviously, the degree of relevance of the inferences depends on the relevance of the theory and on the relevance of the device.

How to evaluate the role and the weight of the "already there"?   We know that both the subject's past social and cognitive experience(s) and representations, concerning the partner and/or the task to solve, play a fundamental role in the nature of the exchanges, within a co-resolution sequence of a problem: but how to study the impact of these experience(s) and representations during the conversation? How to know whether the tools, procedures and strategies used by the subjects are consequences of the luggage "already there" or whether they are built *in situ*? How to appreciate their consequences regarding the final product of the transaction?

How to understand the logical organization of a conversation?   We know that exchanges, the size and composition of which represent basic units of the transaction, are connected linearly and/or hierarchically. Indeed, it is very interesting to abstract logical *structures* from these transactions. But there new questions are asked, which are further limits to the validity of the analysis. How to extract the structures without ambiguity? Does the structure(s) inferred by the researcher correspond to the "true" structure of the conversation? Do structures formally similar "convey" the same significance?

How to estimate (if progress is noticed!) the origin of progress in children?   Lastly, for the researcher who wants to measure subsequent progress in children and to consider that this progress is a consequence of the interaction observed, two main questions emerge: the first one concerns the tool to be used and the second concerns the real nature of the cognitive construction, if it is proven that some progress was accomplished.

CONCLUSION

Beyond the difficulties and limitations we will discuss below, a logical analysis of the interlocution appears as a relevant methodological tool to the understanding of socio-cognitive interactive processes. This has been certified by various studies in the field of educational psychology or developmental psychology (see, for example, Bernicot & Trognon, 2002; Bernicot, Trognon, & Caron-Pargue, 1997; Gilly et al., 1999; Roux, 1999, 2003; Sorsana, 2001, 2003; Sorsana & Marro, 2003; Trognon, 1999, 2003; Trognon & Batt, 2003). Moreover, it has also been validated in several other fields, such as professional situations, political debates or therapeutic settings (see, for example, Bernicot, Trognon, Guidetti & Musiol, 2002; Gilly et al., 1999; Trognon, 1999).

In the field of cognitive developmental psychology, and particularly in the domain of apprenticeship, one can consider that this theory is the best methodological tool to study how interlocutory dynamics produce *simultaneously* inter- and intra-individual mechanisms of social and cognitive phenomena, and overall:

- to describe the genesis and the organization of the socio-cognitive events within the interlocutory process, thanks to *semiotic mediations* "conveyed" through speech acts;
- to understand the process of the construction of *intersubjectivity* (i.e., of a common meaning) as a social product of the cognitive accomplishment of the transaction, object of the conversation between two (or more) interlocutors; and

- to understand the effect of the exchanges on cognition, i.e., to explain why and how the interlocutory dynamic can produce simultaneously inter- and intra-individual mechanisms regarding both social and cognitive phenomena.

REFERENCES

Armengaud, F. (1993). *La pragmatique*. Paris: Presses Universitaires de France. (First edition, 1985).

Austin, J. L. (1962). *How to do things with words*. Oxford, UK: Oxford University Press.

Bernicot, J., & Trognon, A. (2002). Le tournant pragmatique en psychologie. In J. Bernicot, A. Trognon, M. Guidetti, & M. Musiol, *Pragmatique et psychologie* (pp. 73–89). Nancy, France: Presses Universitaires de Nancy.

Bernicot, J., Trognon, A., & Caron-Pargue, J. (1997). *La conversation: Aspects sociaux et cognitifs*. Nancy, France: Presses Universitaires de Nancy.

Bernicot, J., Trognon, A., Guidetti, M., & Musiol, M. (2002). *Pragmatique et psychologie*. Nancy, France: Presses Universitaires de Nancy.

Bronckart, J. P. (1997). Action, discours et rationalisation. L'hypothèse développementale de Vygotski revisitée. In C. Moro, B. Schneuwly, & M. Brossard (Eds.), *Outils et signes. Perspectives actuelles de la théorie de Vygotski* (pp. 199–221). Berne, Switzerland: Peter Lang.

Bronckart, J. P. (2000). *Les processus de socialisation. Le déterminisme culturel et son dépassement*. Paper within the symposium "New conditions of knowledge production: Globalization and social practices". Third Conference for sociocultural research, Sao Paulo, Brésil.

Ghiglione, R., & Trognon, A. (1993). *Où va la Pragmatique?* Grenoble, France: Presses Universitaires de Grenoble.

Gilly, M., Roux, J. P., & Trognon, A. (1999). Apprendre dans l'interaction: pour une analyse dynamique des séquences interactives. Introduction. In M. Gilly, J. P. Roux, & A. Trognon (Eds.), *Apprendre dans l'interaction. Analyse des médiations sémiotiques* (pp. 9–39). Nancy, France: Presses Universitaires de Nancy et Aix: Publications de l'Université de Provence.

Kerbrat-Orecchioni, C. (1990). *Les interactions verbales* (Vol. 1). Paris, France: Armand Colin.

Marro-Clément, P., Trognon, A., & Perret-Clermont, A. N. (1999). Processus interlocutoires dans une tâche de conservation des liquides. In M. Gilly, J. P. Roux, & A. Trognon (Eds.), *Apprendre dans l'interaction. Analyse des médiations sémiotiques* (pp. 163–180). Nancy, France: Presses Universitaires de Nancy et Aix: Publications de l'Université de Provence.

Roulet, E., Auchlin, A., Moeschler, J., Rubattel, C., & Schelling, M. (Eds.). (1991). *L'articulation du discours en français contemporain*. Berne, Switzerland: Peter Lang.

Roux, J. P. (1999). Contexte interactif d'apprentissage en mathématiques et régulation de l'enseignant. In M. Gilly, J. P. Roux, & A. Trognon (Eds.), *Apprendre dans l'interaction. Analyse des médiations sémiotiques* (pp. 259–278). Nancy, France: Presses Universitaires de Nancy et Aix: Publications de l'Université de Provence.

Roux, J. P. (2001a). Theory of interlocutory logic and sequential analysis of interactive problem-solving situations: A powerful method. *Learning Environment Research, 3*, 247–264.

Roux, J. P. (2001b). Analyse interlocutoire d'une situation dyadique de co-résolution de problèmes par des enfants de 5–6 ans. *Psychologie de l'interaction, 13–14*, 315–356.

Roux, J. P. (2003, August). *The interlocutory logic analysis as a methodological approach in studying semiotic mediations: Interest, difficulties, limits*. Paper within the symposium "Dynamics of interlocution and cognitive development" (Chairs C. Sorsana & P. Marro). 11th European Conference on Developmental Psychology, Mailand, Italy.

Roux, J. P. (2007). *Échanges cognitivo-langagiers et appropriation individuelle d'outils cognitifs en situation asymétrique de co-résolution d'une tâche spatiale*. Actes du 3ème colloque international "Constructivisme et éducation: construction intra/intersubjectivité des connaissances et du sujet connaissant". Genève, Suisse.

Roux, J. P., & Froment, M. (2004, March–April). *Working in group at school, speech acts, semiotic mediations and inferences about psychological processes*. Colloque IADA "Theoretical Approaches to Dialogue Analysis", Northeastern Illinois University, Chicago, Illinois, USA.

Searle, J. (1972). *Les actes de langage: Essai de philosophie du langage*. Paris: Hermann. (Original work published 1972).

Searle, J. R., & Vanderveken, D. (1985). *Foundations of illocutionary logic*. Cambridge, UK: Cambridge University Press.

Sorsana, C. (2001). Dynamiques sociales et cognitives des acquisitions. In C. Golder & D. Gaonac'h (Eds.), *Enseigner à des adolescents Manuel de Psychologie* (pp. 208–233). Paris: Hachette.

Sorsana, C. (2003). Comment l'interaction co-opérative rend-elle plus "savant"? Quelques réflexions concernant les conditions nécessaires au fonctionnement dialogique du conflit socio-cognitif. *L'Orientation Scolaire et Professionnelle, 32*(3), 437–473.

Sorsana, C., & Marro, P. (2003, August). *Dynamics of interlocution and cognitive development*. Symposium within the XIth European Conference on Developmental Psychology, Mailand, Italy.

Trognon, A. (1999). Eléments d'analyse interlocutoire. In M. Gilly, J. P. Roux, & A. Trognon (Eds.), *Apprendre dans l'interaction. Analyse des médiations sémiotiques* (pp. 69–94). Nancy, France: Presses Universitaires de Nancy et Aix, Publications de l'Université de Provence.

Trognon, A. (2001). Speech acts and the logic of mutual understanding. In D. Vanderveken & S. Kubo (Eds.), *Essays in speech act theory* (pp. 121–133). Amsterdam: J. Benjamins.

Trognon, A. (2003). La logique interlocutoire: Un programme pour l'étude empirique des jeux de dialogue. *Questions de communication, 4,* 411–425.

Trognon, A., & Batt, M. (2003). L'élaboration et l'appropriation des cognitions dans l'interlocution ou comment représenter le passage de l'intersubjectif à l'intrasubjectif en logique interlocutoire. *L'Orientation Scolaire et Professionnelle, 32*(3), 399–436.

Trognon, A., & Kostulski, K. (1999). Eléments d'une théorie sociocognitive de l'interaction conversationnelle. *Psychologie Française, 44*(4), 307–318.

Trognon, A., Saint-Dizier de Almeida, V., & Grossen, M. (1999). Résolution conjointe d'un problème arithmétique. In M. Gilly, J. P. Roux, & A. Trognon (Eds.), *Apprendre dans l'interaction. Analyse des médiations sémiotiques* (pp. 121–141). Nancy, France: Presses Universitaires de Nancy et Aix: Presses de l'Université de Provence.

Vanderveken, D. (1988). *Les actes de discours*. Liège, Belgium: Mardaga.

Vanderveken, D. (1999). La structure logique des dialogues intelligents. In B. Moulin, S. Delisle, & B. Chaib-Draa (Eds.), *Analyse et simulation. des conversations. de la théorie des actes de discours aux systèmes multiagents, Collection Informatique, L'Interdisciplinaire*, 70–100.

Vanderveken, D., & Kubo, S. (2001). *Essays in speech act theory*. Amsterdam: J.Benjamins.

Vygotski, L. S. (1985). Le problème de l'enseignement et du développement mental à l'âge scolaire. In B. Shneuwly & J. P. Bronckart (Eds.), *Vygotski aujourd'hui* (pp. 95–117). Paris: Delachaux et Niestlé. (Original publication 1933).

Vygotski, L. S. (1985). *Pensée et langage*. Paris: Editions sociales. (Original publication 1934).

Wertsch, J. V. (1985). La médiation sémiotique de la vie mentale: L. S. Vygotsky et M. M. Bakhtine. In B. Schneuwly & J. P. Bronckart (Eds.), *Vygotsky aujourd'hui* (pp. 139–168). Paris: Delachaux et Niestlé.

Wertsch, J. V., & Sanmarco, J. G. (1988). Précurseurs sociaux du fonctionnement cognitif individuel: le problème des unités d'analyse. In R. A. Hinde, A. N. Perret-Clermont, & J. Stevenson-Hinde (Eds.), *Relations interpersonnelles et développement des savoirs* (pp. 395–414). Cousset, France: Delval.

EUROPEAN JOURNAL OF DEVELOPMENTAL PSYCHOLOGY
2008, 5 (5), 623–643

Peer interaction and problem solving: One example of a logical-discursive analysis of a process of joint decision making

Alain Trognon
University of Nancy 2, Nancy, France

Christine Sorsana
University of Toulouse 2, Toulouse, and University of Nancy 2, Nancy, France

Martine Batt
University of Nancy 2, Nancy, France

Dominique Longin
IRIT, University of Toulouse 1, Toulouse, France

This article proposes a qualitative analysis of a dialogue between two children solving the Tower of Hanoi problem. We know that in some circumstances, two heads are better than one. The question is how interactional constraints are likely to provide cognitive benefits? To carry out such an analysis, we use Interlocutory Logic, which is a formal system constructed to express the logical and phenomenological properties of natural conversation. More particularly, we showed how this logical analysis of the interlocution can formalise the socio-cognitive conflict that appears to be an essential "ingredient" of cognitive development from the socio-constructivist perspective.

Keywords: Peer interaction; Problem solving; Conversation; Interlocutory logic.

Correspondence should be addressed to Alain Trognon, Nancy-Université (Nancy 2), Groupe de Recherche sur les Communications (GRC), Département de Psychologie, B.P. 3397, F-54015 Nancy cedex. E-mail: Alain.Trognon@univ-nancy2.fr

This article comes from work carried out within a workshop co-ordinated by Sorsana and Trognon at the University of Nancy 2 (during 2002, 2003 and 2004) and entitled "Analytic methodological constraints of the cognitive production of a conversation". This workshop was subsidized by the Scientific Counsel of the University of Nancy 2 as well as by the "Psychology of interaction – GRC" laboratory (EA 1129) of the same university.

We would like to thank Ciarán O'Keeffe and Maryse Noté for their help with the translation into English.

http://www.psypress.com/edp   DOI: 10.1080/17405620701860165

More and more studies show that when children are confronted with a problem to resolve (e.g., a school evaluation, a psychological test, etc.) their responses depend, among other things, on their conversational interpretation of the questions asked by the adult and, therefore, of the goals this adult assigns to illocutions (Bernicot & Trognon, 2002; Perret-Clermont, Schubauer-Leoni, & Trognon, 1992; Politzer, 1993; Siegal, 1991). For example, studies have shown that the administering of Piagetian tests runs counter to certain general pragmatic principles that perplex the child and conceal his true skills (Light, Gorsuch, & Newman, 1987; Light & Perret-Clermont, 1989; McGarrigle & Donaldson, 1975). In other words, children, and more generally any cognitive subject, are not "monads". They interact permanently with their environment and in particular with other subjects, including the experimenter thereby entering into a full dialogue (Perret-Clermont et al., 1992). "Accounting for this interaction, and especially for the verbal interaction, which is probably the most elaborate, constitutes an essential challenge for cognitive psychology" (Caron, 1997, p. 234). In addition, contrary to adult/child asymmetrical interactions, interactions between peers—when they do not introduce any initial asymmetry—appear to be a privileged place for understanding the meaning of the task that the child progressively constructs (Grossen, 1994).

The studies of the interpersonal forms of learning, initiated by Doise, Mugny, and Perret-Clermont (1975), led to the proposal of a psychosocial model of cognition development (see also Doise & Mugny, 1997; Mugny, 1991; Perret-Clermont, 1996). This is the structuralist model of socio-cognitive conflict. It accounts for the fact that, under certain conditions, working in pairs produces individual cognitive progress greater than that of an individual working alone. "Something" happens, therefore, in the inter-personal interaction that could provide the beginning of an empirical model of Vygotsky's (1962) idea. According to Vygotsky the construction of new interpersonal co-ordination is accomplished thanks to the internalization of inter-personal co-ordination. The analysis by researchers of the procedural approach enabled the characterisation of this "inter-personal co-ordination" hypothesis in describing the actions that are *effectively* carried out by the partners working together (Blaye, 1989, 2001; Dalzon, 2001; Gilly, 1990, 1991, 1995; Gilly & Roux, 1988; Roux & Gilly, 2001; Zhou, 2001). They have shown that the separate actions of the protagonists organize themselves into procedural sequences of resolution. In other words "they co-ordinate themselves to become a sequential cognitive procedure" (Gilly, 1989, p. 497). Thus, in certain conditions, children can go beyond the interdependence (Deutsch, 1949, 1962) arising from reciprocal control of actions while developing a collective intentionality (Dascal, 1992; Searle, 1991).

A new step in the knowledge of the role of interactions in acquisition was made when researchers became attentive to utterances considered also as actions besides the resolution processes of those interacting (Perret-Clermont et al., 1992; Trognon, 1992). The objective of contemporary analysis is to identify the conversational "materials" that denote (even constitute) knowledge-building operations (Gilly, Roux, & Trognon, 1999; Trognon & Batt, 2003; Trognon, Batt, Schwarz, Perret-Clermont, & Marro, 2003). This identification is made on the basis of a formal system—interlocutory logic—conceived to express the logical properties of natural conversation, while respecting its phenomenological properties (Trognon, 1999, 2001, 2003; Trognon & Batt, 2003, 2004, 2007a, 2007b; Trognon, Batt, Schwarz, Perret-Clermont, & Marro, 2006; Trognon & Coulon, 2001; Trognon & Kostulski, 1999). The interlocutory logic theory thus proposes an analysis of the socio-cognitive production of a conversation. Analyses that made explicit the emergence of diverse knowledge in interactions, taking place within the framework of interlocutory logic, have been published over the last few years. These include the following: (1) knowledge pertaining to the correct placement of a cursor during a word-processing tutorial (Trognon & Saint-Dizier, 1999); (2) knowledge pertaining to the handling of a pneumatic drill during learning in the context of an alternance vocational training system (Sannino, Trognon, & Dessagne, 2003; Sannino, Trognon, Dessagne, & Kostulski, 2001); (3) during liquid conservation tasks (Marro, Trognon, & Perret-Clermont, 1999); (4) during educational learning: number division (Trognon, Saint-Dizier de Almeida, & Grossen, 1999) and proportionality (Trognon et al., 2003, 2006b); (5) during hypothetical deductive reasoning applied to an empirical problem (Trognon & Batt, 2003), to a logic problem (Trognon & Batt, 2004) or to a diagnostic procedure (Brixhe, Saint-Dizier, & Trognon, 2000). After presenting interlocutory logic, the present study examines the co-resolution of the Tower of Hanoi problem by two children.

INTERLOCUTORY LOGIC

Interlocutory logic is a theory of the logical form of interlocutory events as they occur phenomenologically. That is to say, as they occur with natural language whose sequential production is distributed between several interlocutors (Trognon & Batt, 2007c; Trognon, Batt, & Laux, 2006a). As a formal theory, it constitutes a system of logical methods selected for their capacity to reflect the phenomenological property of the interlocution. Thus, for example, interlocutory logic will resort preferentially to dialogical methods and to natural deduction methods or those derived from them, like the sequent method.[1] The ambition of interlocutory logic is to provide a natural logic of the usage of speech in interaction.

---

[1]A very accessible presentation of these methods can be found in Vernant (2001).

Interlocutory logic is a theory of dialogue movement in its context

More technically, to analyse an interlocution fragment in interlocutory logic amounts to decomposing this fragment into a series of utterances. Each utterance is represented by an expression ɸ of the system:

$$M_i, \{M_{i-k}\}, \{M_{i-k}\} \vdash M_i, RD, DG$$

M_i is the conversational move accomplished by the utterance under examination. $\{M_{i-k}\}$ is the set of all the conversational moves that precede the move M_i and from which M_i follows. M_i can then be conceived as a *conclusion* that results from *premises* $\{M_{i-k}\}$. The reasoning that leads from $\{M_{i-k}\}$ to M_i, and that is represented by the schema $\{M_{i-k}\} \vdash M_i$, is called, in logic, a sequent.[2]

Let's specify this notion more precisely by adapting an analysis proposed by Carlson (1983).[3] Suppose that A goes to the stadium to attend a pole-vaulting final between Jack and Bob. Delayed, he only arrives at the stadium once the competition has finished. When arriving A entertains the following "ideas": If someone won it is Jack or Bob and someone has won. Moreover, he asks *himself*, "Who has won?" Catching sight of his friend B, he engages in the following dialogue:

1A: *Has Jack won?* (1)
2B: *No.* (2)
3A: *Then Bob won.* (3)
4B: *No.* (4)
5A: *But then nobody won!* (5)

Statement (2) is a response to (1). The rule (or rules; RD) of dialogue (DG) allowing *the derivation of* (2) from (1) is represented by the sequent {1A} ⊢ 2B. The rules that lead from the premise to the conclusion are the questioned rules of semantics exposed in the research of Hintikka (1976, 1984, 1994) of whom Carlson was a student. Statement (3) comes from the "thoughts" entertained by A[4] and from the information 2B worked out

---

[2]A "sequent" is a pair (note $\Gamma \vdash F$) where: Γ is a *finite* set of formulas. Γ represents the hypotheses that one can use. This set is also called the sequent context; - F is a formula. It is the formula that one wants to demonstrate. This formula is said to be the *conclusion* of the "sequent" (David, Nour, & Raffalli, 2003, p. 24).

[3]Even in his recent publications (e.g., 1996) Carlson does not refer to the logic theory of sequents. We think nevertheless that his theory calls for this extension.

[4]This is the *cognitive environment* of A defined by Sperber and Wilson (1995).

together by the logic rule of the disjunctive dilemma.[5] Statement (5) is again deduced from the thoughts entertained by A and from 4B in using *reductio ad absurdum*.

In a relatively informal yet sufficient manner for understanding the meaning of our approach, the previous short dialogue has just been reproduced as the product of a set of dialogue rules formulated as sequents. Some of these rules belong to (dialogical forms of) standard logic. This is the case with the disjunctive dilemma or the classic *reductio ad absurdum* rule, which would be used to demonstrate 5A. Other rules concern, instead, the semantics and pragmatics of natural language. We call *sequents of dialogue* the setting of the relationship in a set of dialogical events (Trognon & Batt, 2007c; Trognon et al., 2006b). This relationship is an inference composed, on the one hand, from a set of premises given in the dialogue and, on the other hand, of events that are deduced from these premises. The rules intervening in this inference are rules of a dialogue game. For example, the dialogue sequent $\{1A\} \vdash 2B$ rests on a rule belonging to the game theory of the question–response dialogue. This example shows that interlocutory logic seems to generalize the sequent notion to all the illocutory acts used in an interlocution.

The internal composition of the movement of a dialogue

From the viewpoint of its internal composition, a move M_i is an expression of the system[6]: $<F(P)>$. F is the force of the speech act accomplished by uttering the utterance. $F = <f_1, f_2, f_3, f_4>$. Where f_1 is the force literally expressed, f_2 the indirect force of the act (if it occurs), f_3 the implicatures of the act, and f_4 the conversational function of the act.[7] We anticipate a little bit the interlocutory analysis that follows, but let us consider, for example, the utterance 12Au that has been emitted by Audrey while she is interacting with Vanessa:

   2Au: *on the brown (disc b)*

---

[5] p v q, or ~p, so q.

[6] Interlocutory logic integrates general semantics (Searle & Vanderveken, 1985; Vanderveken, 1990) as one of its most fundamental components.

[7] f_2, f_3, f_4 are not given simultaneously in the discourse. They result from a process of sharing the inter-comprehension, which transforms the "meaning of the locutor" into the "interlocutors' meaning" (Clark, 1996, 1999), according to a process described in Trognon (2003), Trognon and Brassac (1992), and Trognon and Saint Dizier (1999). The formula that describes, in interlocutory logic, the different levels (from the utterance to the direct act, from the direct act to the indirect act, from the indirect act to the conversational move) of the interpretative genesis of the sign-for-interlocutors is borrowed from Jones (1983). For more detail see Trognon and Batt (2007b), Trognon, Batt, and Laux (2006a).

This elliptic utterance (in fact, it is only a Prepositional Group) is literally an assertive and, non literally, a directive as well as a commissive speech act (because a commissive act is a directive act that the speaker aims at himself). Its conversational function in the interlocution within a framework of problem resolution is (1) to make a proposal for a joint action and (2), in consequence, to refuse the joint action suggested by Vanessa in the preceding speech turn.

P is the propositional content of the speech act that realises the move M_i. This propositional content is described by expressions of the quantified modal first-order predicate logic.[8] For example, the propositional content of 12Au is the modal expression presented below, which describes a future action of the children.

12Au: E_a {[shall E_{v+a} (Awb)]}

E_a: means the (E) action achieved by Audrey (a). The propositional content of this action: [shall E_{v+a} (Awb)], with the Awb formula, which means *white disc on brown disc on peg A*, is describing a state of the world (Awb) that will be realized in the future ("shall" is the modal marker of the future) by the joint action of the two girls, Vanessa and Audrey (E_{v+a}).

A simplified way to write the propositional content of this action is (Awb) if we identify Audrey's proposal with the goal that she aims at when she is uttering, "On the peg A white on brown". Moreover, because (Awb) $\supset \neg$(Bwp) is likely to be a mutual knowledge between the two girls, with the Bwp formula, which means *white disc on pink disc on peg B*, consequently the (Awb) proposal amounts to declining (Bwp), which is Vanessa's proposal.

In the calculations of interlocutory logic, the forces of speech acts are processed as modalities. An utterance like 12Au will therefore be written: *Directive* (Awb). If we assume that the laws of general semantics (Vanderveken, 1990) belong to the speakers' mutual knowledge while they talk together, then the logical expression *Directive* (Awb) $\supset$ To *Desire* (Awb) belongs to the speakers' mutual knowledge too, as well as the *To Desire* (Awb) propositional attitude, thanks to *Modus Ponens*. As a result, the partners both gain access to (at least) one world w_{av} in which Vanessa's desire is satisfied, that is to say a world in which (Awb) is true. In this case, w_{av} is just the content of Audrey and Vanessa's mutual desire. It's an alternative of the real world w_0, which is the world in which Audrey and

---

[8]"Quantified modal first-order predicate logic" was amended, as suggested by Hintikka, in order to adapt it to the "natural logic of the discourse". The connectors of interlocutory logic are the connectors of Hintikka's semantic games (Hintikka & Kulas, 1983). But presentation of this complication is unnecessary in the present study.

Vanessa desire (Awb). The expressions of w_{av} are therefore the expressions of w_0 relieved of their modalities. In interlocutory logic, an expression of this kind is called *a formula reduced to the propositional content of the speech act*. This reduction, legitimate when the dialogue is entirely co-operative, allows the analysis to focus on the dialogue's conceptual content.

THE SOLVING OF THE TOWER OF HANOI PROBLEM BY CHILDREN

Anticipation and planning abilities in children

Research on children solving the Tower of Hanoi problem does not provide consistent results. According to Byrnes and Spitz (1979), planning appears to be very rare before 7–8 years old and only becomes widespread from 14 years old upwards. The problem with two discs is achieved by almost all the subjects as early as 8 years old. The problem with three discs is only successfully solved with the minimum number of moves by 70% of adolescents aged 14 and over. There is rapid progress between 7 and 9 years of age, a plateau between 9 and 12, again important progress between 12 and 14 and, once again, a plateau. These results are in accordance with the different resolution stages reported by Piaget (1974) who placed children in front of an increasing number of discs to move.

This line of research was resumed and disputed by Klahr (1976) and Klahr and Robinson (1981). Using problems with gradual increases in difficulty, the authors showed that children of 5–6 years of age presented rudimentary forms of recursive type planning. This planning involved the working out of goals, the detection of obstacles that would prevent the realization of these goals and the detection of rules indicating the conduct to adopt in this case. These subjects would not develop only trial and error behaviour but a more sophisticated attitude with non-random choices.

Richard (1982) studied the forms of action organization present in the solving of the three discs problem with 495 children aged 7 (tested individually). The following are the principal results:

- The frequency of the correct choices increases when children approach the goal, but there is a lack of continuity. A significant proportion of children (0.42 in the first attempt; 0.31 in the second) do not reach the goal and a minimal proportion of children attain it with the minimum number of moves (0.06 in the first attempt; 0.16 in the second). Even in subjects who do not reach the goal in seven moves, the first move (a deciding factor for the remainder of the problem) does not seem to be the object of any planning that would aim to liberate the larger disc as well as position C in order to be able to move disc 1 onto it.

- Interruptions are observed in the research behaviour (stopping, attempted illegal moves, steps backwards) and these typically happen at certain positions: 55% of the subjects have at least two experimenter interventions in the first attempt for violation of the instructions or stopping completely, and 26% in the second attempt.
- There is a series of positions, of which the preceding ones are a subset where subjects systematically avoid making correct choices. It all happens as if, for them, it was about overcoming a series of obstacles.

Consequently, for Richard (1982), planning[9] intercedes only in a rather late stage of the resolution and corresponds to a transformation of the problem representation. This transformation is motivated by the failure of rules elicited by early problem representations and results in taking into account crucial aspects of the situation that were neglected up till then.

Richard and Poitrenaud (1988; see also Richard, 1990, 1991) subsequently proposed a modelling of this problem solving. It represents research processes that are missing planning, in the strictest sense of the word. These research processes appear to be, according to the authors, characteristic of new situations where it is not possible to find an analogical situation in memory that could serve as a reference point. The authors define three processes:

1. *The representation state*, expressed in the form of hierarchical constraints that are either real constraints of the situation or are imagined by the subject (inappropriate interpretation of the instructions and procedures, goals, rules of action that result).
2. *The construction processes of the state of representation* corresponding to:
   a. *The memorization rules*
   b. *The production rules of the goals*
3. The third process *corresponds to the action and control rules.*

The solving of the Tower of Hanoi problem in dyadic situations

Glachan and Light (1982), and Light and Glachan (1985), used wooden material, including discs with handles, while Light, Foot, Colbourn, and

---

[9]For Richard (1988), planning, in the strictest sense of the word, occurs: either "when the actions necessary to satisfy the instructions can be calculated by action calculation rules but when their execution must be delayed because other constraints must be taken into account to determine the actions' sequential layout"; or "when the situation and the knowledge about the actions is such that other action calculation rules are required to satisfy the task demands" (p. 35). He describes different forms of planning.

McClelland (1987), and Light and Foot (1987), programmed this task on a computer. These studies were aimed at children aged 7 to 9 years old and included the same experimental paradigm (pre-test/training/post-test).

The results, with the wooden material, showed that the "dyadic" condition, with participants of similar initial skills, produces significantly better results than the "individual" condition. Nevertheless, the high-performing dyads are the ones that have children who had shown a strategic approach during the pre-test. A closer examination of the possible causes of observed dyadic results showed that regardless of the type of material, only the interactional modality that forced the children to move the discs together produced significant improvements in the post-test. Performance in two other modalities, one where children are not told to move the discs together and another where the experimenter guided each dyad about the optimal sequence for placement without explanation or justification, was significantly lower. In any case, when children used the "computer" version in the same manner as the wooden one, the peer facilitator effect was less prominent than with the wooden material.

INTERLOCUTORY LOGIC OF A SEQUENCE OF CO-RESOLUTION

The conversational sequence from which the logic form will be constructed is taken from a recording of a dyad of children who are in the process of solving the Tower of Hanoi problem with four discs (cf. Figure 1).

This dyad, of Vanessa and Audrey, comes from a sample of 44 dyads of children aged 6 to 8 participating in research the objective of which was to study the effect of the quality of children's relationship on their cognitive performance. More precisely, it was to study how some non-cognitive

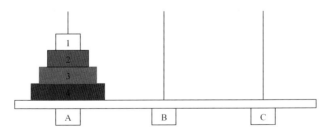

Figure 1. The Tower of Hanoi problem with four discs.

determinants, here the affinity,[10] shape particular behaviours that could result in a specific form of cognitive management at the point at which the Tower of Hanoi problem, with four discs, is solved (Sorsana, 1996, 1997, 1999; Sorsana & Musiol, 2005). The experimental apparatus is standard: pre-test (towers with three discs)/social interaction (with two attempts of co-resolution with four discs)/post-tests (towers with three and four discs). To coerce the children into interacting, the discs were made heavier and they were equipped with handles. Furthermore, the instructions given demand that every disc is moved *together* and stipulates: "Be careful: to move the discs well it is necessary that you look for the solution together, talk it over together and reach an agreement".

The comparison of the "affinity" and "no-affinity" dyads, for the second attempt only, showed a difference in performance and duration of the task depending on the type of dyad: the "affinity" dyads performed better than the "no-affinity" dyads ($z = -2.424$, $p = .007$) and were quicker ($z = -1.908$, $p = .02$). In the post-test with four discs, there was a significant difference between the subjects' performances, in favour of the "affinity" subjects ($z = -1.652$, $p = .04$) with similar task durations ($z = -1.393$, $p = .08$). In the post-test with three discs the differences were not significant.

Only three dyads succeeded in one of the two attempts to rebuild the tower with four discs using the minimum number of moves (i.e., 15). The Vanessa/Audrey dyad was one of them. In addition, the children who were part of this dyad appreciated each other (i.e., it was an "affinity" dyad). The first attempt was accomplished in 35 moves and in 661 seconds. The second attempt was accomplished with an optimum score (15 moves) in 122 seconds. Initially, these two subjects had failed the pre-test (i.e., the reconstruction of the tower with three discs). In the post-test with 4 discs, Vanessa rebuilt the tower in 16 moves and 60 seconds; Audrey in 24 moves and 120 seconds. In the post-test with 3 discs, Vanessa accomplished an optimum score (7 moves) in 60 seconds and Audrey, 9 moves in 60 seconds also. For the children in this dyad, interaction will obviously have been beneficial on the cognitive level.

The choice of this sequence is motivated by the examination of the interlocutory processes employed in order to resolve contradictions that are unavoidably generated by the achievement of a collective intentionality. These contradictions present themselves as socio-cognitive conflicts (cf. Doise & Mugny, 1997; Doise et al., 1975; Gilly, 1990, 1991, 1995; Mugny,

---

[10]Through the use of a sociometric questionnaire, aimed at children, and a standardized interview with the teachers, we selected pairs of children that appreciated each other (which we called "affinity" pairs in reference to the work of Maisonneuve, 1966) and pairs of children that did not appreciate each other (called "no-affinity" pairs).

1991; Perret-Clermont, 1996). These conflicts are, one the one hand, cognitive conflicts: the children's strategies are contradictory; they share the same goal, but can disagree on how to attain it (i.e., on the sequencing of the subgoals that the task seems to impose on them). These conflicts are also, on the other hand, social, perhaps even emotional, conflicts. The one who wins over the argument in a conflict of responses occurring within a close relationship causes their partner to lose face. Consequently they endure the dissonance of infringing upon friendship obligations in wanting the dyad to succeed. The interactional "cost" of a socio-cognitive conflict, then, seems higher within an affinity dyad than within a dyad with no affinity.[11]

To study this conflict of responses within the Vanessa/Audrey dyad, we start by reproducing the sequence within which it appears. We then analyse the internal composition of each utterance. Then, we reveal the (dia)logical structure of the utterances that form the socio-cognitive conflict, from its inauguration in the dialogue until its resolution.

Dialogue extract containing the socio-cognitive conflict

Note: from the smallest one to the biggest one, the colours of the discs of the Tower of Hanoi are: white (w), pink (p), green (g) and brown (b).

1Va: Let's put it (disc w) there (peg B)
2: Co-action
3Va: Let's put it (disc p) there (peg C)
4: Co-action
5Va: After we take the other disc ...
6Va: Let's put it (disc w) there (peg C)
7: Co-action
8Va: Let's put it (disc g) there (peg B)
9: Co-action
10: (Lift up disc w)
11Va: On the green (disc g)
12Au: On the brown (disc b)
13Va1: No
13Va2: On the green
14Au1: No
14Au2: Let's put the pink one there (disc p)
15Va1: Wait, wait
15Va2: (Looks at the experimenter)
15Va3: Let's put it on the green
16Au1: No

---

[11]In game theories (and in particular dialogue game theory), this factor would play a important role (cf. Bromberg & Trognon, 2000, 2004; Hintikka, 1962, 1976, 1984).

16Au2: Afterwards let's put that one there (disc p on disc g using her hand gesture)
17Va1: Yes
17Va2: But we must build the tower there (peg C)
17Va3: Ah yes
17Va4: That's it
18: Co-action (disc w on disc b on peg A)
19: Co-action (disc p on disc g on peg B)
20Va: OK!
21Au: (smiles)

Internal decomposition of the series of dialogue moves contributing to the socio-cognitive conflict

Our analysis concerns the extract (11Va...21Au) that is produced immediately following the lifting up of disc 1 (w) by the two children. This sequence sets the stage for a disagreement between the two children. From this disagreement an inter-comprehension process emerged that then led to an agreement. Even though, from 11Va to 15Va, the disagreement was concerned with the place to put (w), it was Audrey's reasoning, in 14Au and 16Au, that ended up imposing itself as illustrated by what Vanessa expressed in 17Va.

Once the 9 co-action was carried out, the four discs were on the pegs as follows: the brown disc was on peg A, so we write [A(-, -, -, b)], the green disc was on peg B, so we write [B(-, -, -, g)] and the white and pink discs were on peg C, so we write [C(-, -, w, p)]. When several discs are on the same peg, they are written from the smallest one to the biggest one. Thus, the overall configuration of pegs and discs is: [A(-, -, -, b) & B(-, -, -, g) & C(-, -, w, p)].

The different stages followed by the children until the preceding configuration were as follows:

Initial situation: A(w, p, g, b) & B(-, -, -, -) & C(-, -, -, -)
1Va then 2 co-action: A(-, p, g, b) & B(-, -, -, w) & C(-, -, -, -)
3Va then 4 co-action: A(-, -, g, b) & B(-, -, -, w) & C(-, -, -, p)
5−6Va then 7 co-action: A(-, -, g, b) & B(-, -, -, -) & C(-, -, w, p)
8Va then 9 co-action: A(-, -, -, b) & B(-, -, -, g) & C(-, -, w, p)

The girls progressed as if they were following the exact pattern of the recursive model[12] of the resolution of the Tower of Hanoi problem. According to this model: "In order to move *n* discs from peg A to peg C, one

---

[12]The authors hold at the disposal of readers a recursive data-processing model of the children's enacted reasoning.

must necessarily proceed in three stages. The first stage consists in transferring $n - 1$ discs from peg A to peg B, the second stage in transferring one disc (the biggest one) from peg A to peg C and the last stage in transferring $n - 1$ discs from peg B to peg C" (Gochet, Gribomont, & Thayse, 2000, pp. 262–264). By applying this method $n - 1$ times, "one gets the optimal list of the elementary moves" (p. 264); and it's exactly the way that will be followed by Audrey and Vanessa.

The children have two options when they lift up disc w. Either Vanessa and Audrey put it on peg A (on the brown disc): [A(-, -, w, b)]. Or they put it on peg B (on the green disc): [B(-, -, w, g)]. The choice is strategically decisive. The girls have just moved two discs from peg A to peg C and another disc from peg A to peg B. They are therefore very close to reaching an essential subgoal in the solution of the problem: moving three discs from peg A to peg B, then moving a disc from peg A to peg C. Indeed, to reach this state of the world, they only have to proceed from 9 as follows below:

A(-, -, w, b) & B(-, -, -, g) & C(-, -, -, p)
A(-, -, w, b) & B(-, -, p, g) & C(-, -, -, -)
A(-, -, -, b) & B(-, w, p, g) & C(-, -, -, -)
A(-, -, -, -) & B (-, w, p, g) & C(-, -, -, b)

The choice is crucial from two points of view. From a logical standpoint, it is clear that to move the white disc onto the green disc (Vanessa's proposal) is less interesting than to move the white disc onto the brown disc (Audrey's proposal) because, in the latter proposal, then the pink disc may be moved onto the green one, then the white disc onto the pink one, and, finally, the brown disc onto peg C. From a psychological standpoint now, in their modelling of the solution of the problem, Richard and Poitrenaud (1988) and Richard (1990, 1991) demonstrated that in this solving stage the participants (including adults) avoid placing another disc on the larger disc—finally released—and favour the movement of disc w onto the peg B.

From 11Va to 21Au, the children will find the best solution. But they will first have to exceed a socio-cognitive conflict. This conflict develops as follows. From 10 to 13Va$_2$, we attend the installation of the conflict. Each girl states the goal she wants to carry out (11Va *versus* 12Au), then the incompatibility with the partner's goal (13Va$_1$ *versus* 14Au$_1$): the contra-diction of the propositional contents involves an incompatibility of the acts (Searle & Vanderveken, 1985). An argumentative phase follows, more or less superimposed on the preceding phase. During this phase, each player argues her thesis (14Au$_2$–16Au$_2$ *versus* 17Va$_2$). Then, a phase of resolution *may* close the conflict, as in the interaction that we are examining (cf. Table 1), where one of the girls will adopt the option initially suggested by her partner.

TABLE 1

Interlocutory analysis of a disagreement between two children

Sequential verbal exchanges	Illocutory speech acts	Occurrence	Vanessa	Audrey
(...)				
10: (they lift up w)				
11Va: on the green (g)	Directive-commissive	Proposition	B(-, -, w, g)	
12Au: on the brown (b)	Directive-commissive	Proposition		A(-, -, w, b)
13Va₁: no	Assertive	Rejection of 12 Au		¬A(-,-, w, b)
13Va₂: on the green	Directive-commissive	Repetition	B(-, -, w, g)	
14Au₁: no	Assertive	Rejection of 13 Va		¬B(-, -, w, g)
14Au₂: Let's put the pink one (p) there	Assertive	Argument		B(-, -, p, g)
15Va₁: wait, wait	Directive	Request		
15Va₂: (looks at the experimenter)				
15Va₃: let's put it on the green	Directive-commissive	Repetition	B(-, -, w, g)	
16Au₁: no	Assertive	Rejection of 12 Au		¬B(-, -, w, g)
16Au₂: afterwards, let's put that one there (p on g using her hand gesture)	Assertive	Reminder of the justification of the rejection		B(-, -p, g)
17Va₁: yes	Assertive			
17Va₂: but we must build the tower there (peg C)	Assertive	Argument	C(-, -, -)	
17Va₃: ah yes	Expressive	Agreement	¬B(-, -, w, g) + B(-, -, p, g) = C(-, -, -)	
17Va₄: that's it	Assertive	Success and satisfaction of 12Au		
18: (co-action)				
19: (co-action)				
20Va: OK	Expressive	Agreement		
21Va: (smiles)	Expressive	Satisfaction		
(...)				

By calculating her proposal with her partner's proposal taken as an assumption, each girl deduces a contradiction, by a simple reasoning *ad absurdum*. Because the interaction cannot continue on the mode of opposition, except by entering a "dialogue of the deaf" where each interlocutor indefinitely repeats his point of view, alternatively at each turn of speech, the girls must adopt another dialogue game if they wish to prolong their co-operation. Then they engage in a mixed dialogue of argumentation (Rips, 1998; Walton & Krabbe, 1995), in which each player is supposed to persuade her partner by using a battery of strategies. To challenge her partner to argue in favour of her own thesis is one of these strategies. A player receiving a challenge must put forward an argument, otherwise he/she loses the game. In this interaction, no challenge is uttered, but the children put forward their arguments respectively. Examining both the justification put forward by Vanessa ($17Va_2$) and the arguments uttered by Audrey in order to reject Vanessa's proposal ($16Au_1 + 16Au_2$), we notice that the former follows from the latter:

$$(16Au_1 \ \& \ 16Au_2) \rightarrow 17Va_2$$

The dialogue game theory of persuasion (Walton & Krabbe, 1995) demonstrated that a player wins the game when he/she manages to demonstrate his/her thesis starting from the opponent's concessions. If we supposed that Vanessa took Audrey's assertions for assumptions in her own reasoning, then she should deduce $17Va_2$. Consequently, Vanessa hasn't got any more reason to reject Audrey's proposal. Moreover, if Audrey and Vanessa's proposals both lead to the same situation—the release of the peg C—Audrey's proposal remains strategically higher, because it makes it possible to reach a key subgoal of the problem more quickly. And it is subjected to the condition that Vanessa's proposal will be followed by a move of the pink disc onto the brown one, a proposal that has not been uttered by Vanessa (yet?). In any case, the positive relationships between the two girls are likely to support the resolution of the disagreement ($17Va_{3-4}$). Therefore they accomplish Audrey's solution (18–19), and Vanessa approves its accuracy (20Va) to Audrey's satisfaction, which she expresses with her smiles (21Au).

In the analysis that we propose here, on the one hand, Vanessa will not have needed to devote herself to a comparative study of the consequences of both her proposal and Audrey's on the rest of the play to adopt her partner's standpoint: the interest of Audrey's proposal is "staring her in the face". On the other hand, the success of Audrey's strategy, that the children will then test, will reinforce their decision positively. It may be thanks to a contingent interaction like the one that we have just examined that Audrey and Vanessa acquired the solution of the Tower of Hanoi problem.

CONCLUSION

In this article, we have shown how interlocutory logic can formalize the socio-cognitive conflict, which is an essential ingredient of development for the psychology of social genetics "school" (Doise & Mugny, 1997; Doise et al., 1975; Mugny, 1991; Perret-Clermont, 1996).

Until now, interlocutory logic, which is generally meant as a theory on the "logic form" of interlocutions or as a theory of the "natural logic" contained in discourse usage in interaction, has mainly been used to formally demonstrate socio-cognitive events. The interlocutory events in these analyses are taken as conclusions to be inferred in a dialogue system. For example, in the present article, interlocutory logic explains why Vanessa grants Audrey's suggestion while abandoning hers. This amounts to solving the socio-cognitive conflict in which the children were involved. This resolution mode differs from the one considered most effective from the standpoint of cognitive development by the social genetic psychology school. Vanessa's agreement is situated, in effect, between the obliging agreement (compliance) and the integration of two viewpoints in a synthesis that preserves them and exceeds them. What remains is that, even though demonstrative, our (dia)logical explanation constitutes speculation among others. It will only be possible to ascertain it by appealing to the "cutting edge" of experimentation.

Compared to the psychosocial theory of cognitive development, interlocutory logic constitutes a formal improvement because it clarifies the semiotic mediations in which the sequential cognitive procedures are expressed. Interlocutory logic also constitutes a theoretical improvement in so far as the sequential cognitive procedures are rarely given directly in the interaction, that is to say in the "ordinary life" (Trognon, Batt, & Laux, 2007; Trognon & Bromberg, 2008).

Other uses of interlocutory logic are conceivable in developmental psychology. For example: to design a developmental model of interactional competences and their cognitive effects, following up on the works of Bruner (1983, 1986, 1990), Harris (2000) and Tomasello (1999); to better control the situation that constitutes "the uphill struggle" of developmental psychology and all the others; that is, "the indeterminacy of radical translation" (Quine, 1960), of which Piaget was, in his own way, surely acutely aware when he devised the clinical interview (Piaget, 1926).

REFERENCES

Bernicot, J., & Trognon, A. (2002). Le tournant pragmatique en psychologie. In J. Bernicot, A. Trognon, M. Guidetti, & M. Musiol (Eds.), *Pragmatique et psychologie* (pp. 13–32). Nancy, France: Presses Universitaires de Nancy.

Blaye, A. (1989). Interactions sociales et constructions cognitives: présentation critique de la thèse du conflit sociocognitif. In N. Bednarz & C. Garnier (Eds.), *Construction des savoirs: Obstacles et conflits* (pp. 183–194). Montréal, Canada: Agence d'Arc Inc.

Blaye, A. (2001). Mécanismes générateurs de progrès lors de la résolution à deux d'un produit de deux ensembles par des enfants de 5–6 ans. In A. N. Perret-Clermont, & M. Nicolet (Eds.), *Interagir et connaître. Enjeux et régulations sociales dans le développement cognitif* (pp. 49–62). Paris: L'Harmattan. (First edition, 1988).

Brixhe, D., Saint-Dizier, V., & Trognon, A. (2000). Résolution interlocutoire d'un diagnostic. *Psychologie de l'Interaction, 9–10*, 211–237.

Bromberg, M., & Trognon, A. (2000). La psychologie sociale de l'usage du langage. In N. Roussiau (Ed.), *Psychologie sociale* (pp. 293–312). Paris: In press Editions.

Bromberg, M., & Trognon, A. (2004). Introduction. In M. Bromberg & A. Trognon (Eds.), *Psychologie sociale et communication* (pp. 1–15). Paris: Dunod.

Bruner, J. (1983). *Child's talk: Learning to use language.* New York: Norton.

Bruner, J. (1986). *Actual minds, possible worlds.* Cambridge, MA: Harvard University Press.

Bruner, J. (1990). *Acts of meaning.* Cambridge, MA: Harvard University Press.

Byrnes, M. N., & Spitz, H. H. (1979). Developmental progression of performance on the Tower of Hanoi problem. *Bulletin of the Psychonomic Society, 14*(5), 379–381.

Carlson, L. (1983). *Dialogue games. An approach to discourse analysis.* Dordrecht, The Netherlands: Reidel.

Carlson, L. (1996). Language as a Game. In J. L. Mey (Ed.), *Concise encyclopedia of pragmatics* (pp. 447–450). Amsterdam: Elsevier.

Caron, J. (1997). Psychologie cognitive et interactions conversationnelles. In J. Bernicot, J. Caron-Pargue, & A. Trognon (Eds.), *Conversation, interaction et fonctionnement cognitif* (pp. 221–237). Nancy, France: Presses Universitaires de Nancy.

Clark, H. H. (1996). *Using language.* Cambridge, UK: Cambridge University Press.

Clark, H. H. (1999). On the origins of conversation. *Verbum, XXI*(2), 147–161.

Dalzon, C. (2001). Conflit cognitif et construction de la notion Droite/Gauche. In A. N. Perret-Clermont & M. Nicolet (Eds.), *Interagir et connaître. Enjeux et régulations sociales dans le développement cognitif* (pp. 63–78). Paris: L'Harmattan. (First edition, 1988).

Dascal, M. (1992). On the pragmatic structure of conversation. In H. Parret & J. Verschueren (Eds.), *(On) Searle on conversation* (pp. 35–57). Amsterdam: John Benjamins.

David, R., Nour, K., & Raffalli, C. (2003). *Introduction à la logique.* Paris: Dunod.

Deutsch, M. (1949). A theory of cooperation and competition. *Human Relations, 2*, 129–152.

Deutsch, M. (1962). Cooperation and trust: Some theoretical notes. In M. R. Jones (Ed.), *Nebraska symposium on motivation* (pp. 275–320). Lincoln: University of Nebraska Press.

Doise, W., & Mugny, G. (1997). *Le développement social de l'intelligence.* Paris: A. Colin. (First edition, 1981).

Doise, W., Mugny, G., & Perret-Clermont, A. N. (1975). Social interaction and the development of cognitive operations. *European Journal of Social Psychology, 5*, 367–383.

Gilly, M. (1989). Commentaires (du rapport de Jean-Paul Codol "Cognition sociale"). *Bulletin de Psychologie, XLII*(390), 494–497.

Gilly, M. (1990). Mécanismes psychosociaux des constructions cognitives: Perspectives de recherche à l'âge scolaire. In G. Netchine-Grynberg (Ed.), *Développement et fonctionnement cognitif: renouveaux en psychologie de l'enfant* (pp. 201–222). Paris: Presses Universitaires de France.

Gilly, M. (1991). Social psychology of cognitive constructions: European perspectives. In M. Carretero, M. Pope, S. Robertjan, & J. L. Pozo (Eds.), *Learning and instruction. European research in an international context.* (Vol. III, pp. 99–123). Oxford, UK: Pergamon Press.

Gilly, M. (1995). Approches socioconstructives du développement cognitif. In G. Gaonach & C. Golder (Eds.), *Manuel de psychologie pour l'enseignement* (pp. 130–167). Paris: Hachette (Education).

Gilly, M., & Roux, J.-P. (1988). Social marking in ordering tasks: Effects and action mechanisms. *European Journal of Social Psychology, 18,* 251–266.

Gilly M., Roux J.-P., & Trognon A. (Eds.). (1999). *Apprendre dans l'interaction. Analyse des médiations sémiotiques.* Aix-en-Provence et Nancy, France: Presses de l'Université de Provence et Presses Universitaires de Nancy.

Glachan, M., & Light, P. (1982). Peer interaction and learning: Can two wrongs make a right? In G. Butterworth & P. Light (Eds.), *Social cognition* (pp. 238–262). Chicago: University of Chicago Press.

Gochet, P., Gribomont, P., & Thayse, A. (2000). *Logique. Méthodes pour l'intelligence artificielle.* Paris: Hermès.

Grossen, M. (1994). Theoretical and methodological consequences of a change in the unit of analysis for the study of peer interactions in a problem solving situation. *European Journal of Psychology of Education, IX*(1), 159–173.

Harris, P. L. (2000). *The work of the imagination.* Oxford, UK: Blackwell.

Hintikka, J. (1962). *Knowledge and belief. An introduction to the logic of the two notions.* Ithaca, NY: Cornell University Press.

Hintikka, J. (1976). Languages-games. *Acta Philosophica Fennica, 28*(1–3), 105–125. (Essays on Wittgenstein in honour of G. H. Von Wright).

Hintikka, J. (1984). Rules, utilities, and strategies in dialogical games. In L. Vaina & J. Hintikka (Eds.), *Cognitive constraints on communication* (pp. 277–294). Amsterdam: D. Reidel.

Hintikka, J. (1994). *Fondements d'une théorie du langage.* Paris: Presses Universitaires de France.

Hintikka, J., & Kulas, J. (1983). *The game of language. Studies in game theoretical semantics and its applications.* Dordrecht, The Netherlands: D. Reidel.

Jones, A. J. I. (1983). *Communication and meaning. An essay in applied modal logic.* Dordrecht, The Netherlands: D. Reidel.

Klahr, D. (1976). Goal formation, planning and learning by pre-school problem solvers or "my socks are in the dryer". In R. S. Siegler (Ed.), *Children's thinking. What develops?* (pp. 181–212). Hillsdale, NJ: Lawrence Erlbaum Associates, Inc.

Klahr, D., & Robinson, M. (1981). Formal assessment of problem solving and planning processes in preschool children. *Cognitive Psychology, 13,* 113–148.

Light, P., & Foot, T. (1987). Peer interaction and micro-computer use. *Rassegna di Psicologia, 4*(2/3), 93–104.

Light, P., Foot, T., Colbourn, C., & McClelland, I. (1987). Collaborative interactions at the microcomputer keyboard. *Educational Psychology, 7*(1), 13–21.

Light, P., & Glachan, M. (1985). Facilitation of individual problem solving through peer interaction. *Educational Psychology, 5,* 217–225.

Light, P., Gorsuch, C., & Newman, J. (1987). "Why do you ask?" Context and communication in the conservation task. *European Journal of Psychology of Education, II*(1), 73–82.

Light, P., & Perret-Clermont, A.-N. (1989). Social context effects in learning and testing. In A. Gellatly, D. Rogers, & J. A. Sloboda (Eds.), *Cognition and social words* (pp. 99–112). Oxford, UK: Oxford University Press.

Maisonneuve, J. (1966). *Psycho-sociologie des affinités.* Paris: Presses Universitaires de France.

Marro, P., Trognon, A., & Perret-Clermont, A.-N. (1999). Processus interlocutoires dans une tâche de conservation des liquides. In M. Gilly, J. P. Roux, & A. Trognon (Eds.), *Apprendre dans l'interaction: Analyse des médiations sémiotiques* (pp. 163–180). Aix-en-Provence & Nancy, France: Publications de l'Université de Provence & Presses Universitaires de Nancy.

McGarrigle, J., & Donaldson, M. (1975). Conservation accidents. *Cognition, 3*(4), 341–350.

Mugny, G. (1991). *Psychologie sociale du développement cognitif.* Berne, Switzerland: P. Lang. (First edition, 1985).

Perret-Clermont, A. N. (1996). *La construction de l'intelligence dans l'interaction sociale.* Berne, Switzerland: P. Lang. (First edition, 1979).

Perret-Clermont, A. N., Schubauer-Leoni, M. L., & Trognon, A. (1992). L'extorsion des réponses en situation asymétrique. *Verbum, 1–2,* 3–32.

Piaget, J. (1926). *La représentation du monde chez l'enfant.* Paris: Presses Universitaires de France.

Piaget, J. (1974). *La prise de conscience.* Paris: Presses Universitaires de France.

Politzer, G. (1993). *La psychologie du raisonnement: lois de la pragmatique et logique formelle.* Doctorat d'Etat ès Lettres et Sciences Humaines. Université de Paris VIII, Paris.

Quine, W. V. O. (1960). *Word and object.* Cambridge, MA: MIT Press.

Richard, J.-F. (1982). Planification et organisation des actions dans la résolution du problème de la Tour de Hanoi par des enfants de 7 ans. *L'Année Psychologique, 82,* 307–336.

Richard, J.-F. (1988). Les activités de planification chez l'enfant. *Revue Française de Pédagogie, 82,* 33–37.

Richard, J.-F. (1990). *Les activités mentales: comprendre, raisonner, trouver des solutions.* Paris: A. Colin.

Richard, J.-F. (1991). Analyse de procédures et modélisation de la résolution de problème. In G. Vergnaud (Ed.), *Les sciences cognitives en débat* (pp. 29–40). Paris: CNRS Editions.

Richard, J.-F., & Poitrenaud, S. (1988). Problématique de l'analyse des protocoles individuels d'observations comportementales. In J. P. Caverni (Ed.), *Psychologie cognitive, modèles et méthodes* (pp. 405–426). Grenoble, France: Presses Universitaires de Grenoble.

Rips, L. J. (1998). Reasoning and conversation. *Psychological Review, 105*(3), 411–441.

Roux, J.-P., & Gilly, M. (2001). Contribution à l'étude des mécanismes d'action du marquage social dans une tâche d'ordination à 12–13 ans. In A. N. Perret-Clermont & M. Nicolet (Eds.), *Interagir et connaître: Enjeux et régulations sociales dans le développement cognitif* (pp. 171–185). Cousset, France: DelVal. (First edition, 1988).

Sannino, A., Trognon, A., Dessagne, L. (2003). A model for analyzing knowledge content and processes of learning a trade within alternance vocational training. In T. Tuomi-Groh & Y. Engeström (Eds.), *Between school and work: New perspectives on transfer and boundary-crossing* (pp. 271–289). Amsterdam: Pergamon.

Sannino, A., Trognon, A., Dessagne, L., & Kostulski, K. (2001). Les connaissances émergeant d'une relation tuteur-apprenti sur le lieu de travail. *Bulletin de Psychologie, 54*(3), 453, 261–273.

Searle, J. R. (1991). *On Searle on conversation. Pragmatics and beyond.* Amsterdam: John Benjamins.

Searle, J. R., & Vanderveken, D. (1985). *Foundations of illocutionary logic.* Cambridge, UK: Cambridge University Press.

Siegal, M. (1991). A clash of conversational worlds: Interpreting cognitive development through communication. In L. B. Resnick & J. M. L. S. Teasley (Eds.), *Perspectives on socially shared cognition* (pp. 23–41). Washington, DC: American Psychological Association.

Sorsana, C. (1996). Relations affinitaires et co-résolution de problème: analyse des interactions entre enfants de six-huit ans. *Interaction et Cognitions, 2–3,* 263–291.

Sorsana, C. (1997). Affinités enfantines et co-résolution de la Tour de Hanoï. *La Revue Internationale de Psychologie Sociale, 1*, 51–74.

Sorsana, C. (1999). Stratégies sociocognitives dans la résolution de la Tour de Hanoï. In M. Gilly, J. P. Roux, & A. Trognon (Eds.), *Apprendre dans l'interaction. Analyse des médiations sémiotiques* (pp. 143–161). Aix-en-Provence & Nancy, France: Presses de l'Université de Provence & Presses Universitaires de Nancy.

Sorsana, C., & Musiol, M. (2005). Power and knowledge: How can rationality emerge from children's interactions in a problem-solving situation? In E. Grillo (Ed.), *Power without domination, dialogism and the empowering property of communication* (pp. 161–221). Amsterdam: John Benjamins.

Sperber, D., & Wilson, D. (1995). *Relevance. Communication and cognition.* Oxford, UK: Blackwell Publishers. (First edition, 1986).

Tomasello, M. (1999). *The cultural origins of human cognition.* New York: Harvard University Press.

Trognon, A. (1992). Psychologia cognitiva e analisi delle conversazioni. In C. Galimberti (Ed.), *La conversazione. Prospettive sull'interazione psico-sociale* (pp. 115–155). Milan: Guerini Studio.

Trognon, A. (1999). Eléments d'analyse interlocutoire. In M. Gilly, J. P. Roux, & A. Trognon (Eds.), *Apprendre dans l'interaction. Analyse des médiations sémiotiques* (pp. 69–94). Aix-en-Provence & Nancy, France: Publications de l'Université de Provence & Presses Universitaires de Nancy.

Trognon, A. (2001). Speech acts and the logic of mutual understanding. In D. Vanderveken & S. Kubo (Eds.), *Essays in speech act theory* (pp. 121–133). Amsterdam: John Benjamins.

Trognon, A. (2003). La logique interlocutoire: Un programme pour l'étude empirique des jeux de dialogue. *Questions de communication, 4*, 411–425.

Trognon, A., & Batt, M. (2003). L'élaboration et l'appropriation des cognitions dans l'interlocution ou comment représenter le passage de l'Intersubjectif à l'Intrasubjectif en Logique Interlocutoire. *L'Orientation Scolaire et Professionnelle, 32*(3), 399–436.

Trognon, A., & Batt, M. (2004). Logique interlocutoire des jeux de dialogue: Un programme en psychologie sociale de l'usage du langage. In M. Bromberg & A. Trognon (Eds.), *Psychologie sociale et communication* (pp. 135–156). Paris: Dunod.

Trognon, A., & Batt, M. (2007a). A unified framework for studying conversational interaction. In P. J. Thibault & C. Prevignano (Eds.), *Interaction analysis and language: Discussing the state-of-art.* Amsterdam: John Benjamins.

Trognon, A., & Batt, M. (2007b). Quelles méthodes logiques pour l'étude de l'interaction en psychologie. In C. Chabrol, I. Olry-Louis, & F. Najab (Eds.), *Interactions communicatives et psychologies* (pp. 53–65). Paris: Presses de la Sorbonne Nouvelle.

Trognon, A., & Batt, M. (2007c). Comment conduire l'examen d'un fragment d'interlocution au moyen de la logique interlocutoire. In A. Specogna (Ed.), *Enseigner dans l'interaction* (pp. 13–33). Nancy, France: Presses Universitaires de Nancy.

Trognon, A., Batt, M., & Laux, J. (2006a). Logique interlocutoire du problème des quatre cartes posé à une dyade. *Psychologie de l'Interaction, 21–22*, 143–188.

Trognon, A., Batt, M., & Laux, J. (2007). Psychologie sociale et raisonnement. In S. Rossi & J. B. Van der Henst (Eds.), *Psychologies du raisonnement* (pp. 141–166). Bruxelles, Belgium: De Boeck.

Trognon, A., Batt, M., Schwarz, B., Perret-Clermont, A. N., & Marro, P. (2003). L'apprentissage dans l'interaction: Essai d'analyse interlocutoire. In A. Herzig, B. Chaib-Draa, & P. Mathieu (Eds.), *MFI'03 Modèles formels de l'interaction* (pp. 229–240). Toulouse, France: Cépaduès.

Trognon, A., Batt, M., Schwarz, B., Perret-Clermont, A. N., & Marro, P. (2006b). Logique interlocutoire de la résolution en dyade d'un problème d'arithmétique. *Psychologie Française, 51*, 171–187.

Trognon, A., & Brassac, C. (1992). L'enchaînement conversationnel. *Cahiers de linguistique française, 13*, 76–107.

Trognon, A., & Bromberg, M. (2008). L'interaction sociale. In A. Trognon & M. Bromberg (Eds.), *Psychologie sociale et ressources humaines*. Paris: Presses Universitaires de France.

Trognon, A., & Coulon, D. (2001). La modélisation des raisonnements générés dans les interlocutions. *Langages, 144*, 58–77.

Trognon, A., & Kostulski, K. (1999). Eléments d'une théorie sociocognitive de l'interaction conversationnelle. *Psychologie Française, 44*(4), 307–318.

Trognon, A., & Saint-Dizier, V. (1999). L'organisation conversationnelle des malentendus: le cas d'un dialogue tutoriel. *Journal of Pragmatics, 31*, 787–815.

Trognon, A., Saint-Dizier de Almeida, V., & Grossen, M. (1999). Résolution conjointe d'un problème arithmétique. In M. Gilly, J. P. Roux, & A. Trognon (Eds.), *Apprendre dans l'interaction: Analyse des médiations sémiotiques* (pp. 121–141). Aix-en-Provence & Nancy, France: Publications de l'Université de Provence & Presses Universitaires de Nancy.

Vanderveken, D. (1990). *Meaning and speech acts*. Cambridge, UK: Cambridge University Press.

Vernant, D. (2001). *Introduction à la logique standard*. Paris: Flammarion.

Vygotsky, L. S. (1962). *Thought and language*. Cambridge, MA: MIT Press.

Walton, D., & Krabbe, C. W. (1995). *Commitment in dialogue: Basic concepts of interpersonal reasoning*. Albany, NY: State University of New York Press.

Zhou, R. M. (2001). Norme égalitaire, conduites sociales de partage et acquisition de la conservation des quantités. In A. N. Perret-Clermont, & M. Nicolet (Eds.), *Interagir et connaître: Enjeux et régulations sociales dans le développement cognitif* (pp. 187–201). Paris: L'Harmattan. (First edition, 1988).

European Journal of Developmental Psychology
Volume 5, 2008, List of Contents

Issue 5
Special issue—Developmental co-construction of cognition
Guest editor—Christine Sorsana

European Journal of Developmental Psychology
Volume 5, 2008, Author Index

European Journal of Developmental Psychology
Volume 5, 2008, List of Reviewers

The editors and the editorial board would like to thank the following for reviewing papers for the journal from August 2007 to September 2008: